METALHEART

2001 © Anders F Rönnblom and Andreas Lindholm

First published in Japan by
DesignEXchange Company Limited
BR Takanawa 3-12-8 Takanawa Minato-ku Tokyo 108-0074 Japan
Phone:+81 (3) 5798-0216 Fax:+81 (3) 5798-0212
e-mail:pub@dex.ne.jp url:http//www.dex.ne.jp

First published in English by
HBI, an imprint of HarperCollins Publishers
10 East 53rd Street
New York, NY 10022-5299

Distributed exclusively worldwide except Japan, England, and the United States by
HarperCollins International
10 East 53rd Street
New York, NY 10022-5299
Fax: (212) 207-7654

First published in the United States by
Gingko Press Inc.
5768 Paradise Drive, Suite J
Corte Madera CA 94925 USA
Phone: (415) 924-9615 Fax: (415) 924-9608
e-mail: books@gingkopress.com
web: www.gingkopress.com

First published in the UK by Laurence King Publishing
an imprint of Calmann & King Ltd.
71 Great Russell Street
London WC1B 3BP
Phone: +44 (020) 7430-8850 Fax: +44 (020) 7430 8880
e-mail: enquiries@calmann-king.co.uk
web: www.laurence-king.com
ISBN 1 85669 252 3
A catalogue record for this book is available from the British Library.

Cover and book design by Anders F Rönnblom and Andreas Lindholm

Printed in Hong Kong by Everbest Printing Co., Ltd.
First printing, 2001

LOVE
METALHEART IS LOVE

Andreas Lindholm   Anders F Rönnblom

 Laurence King

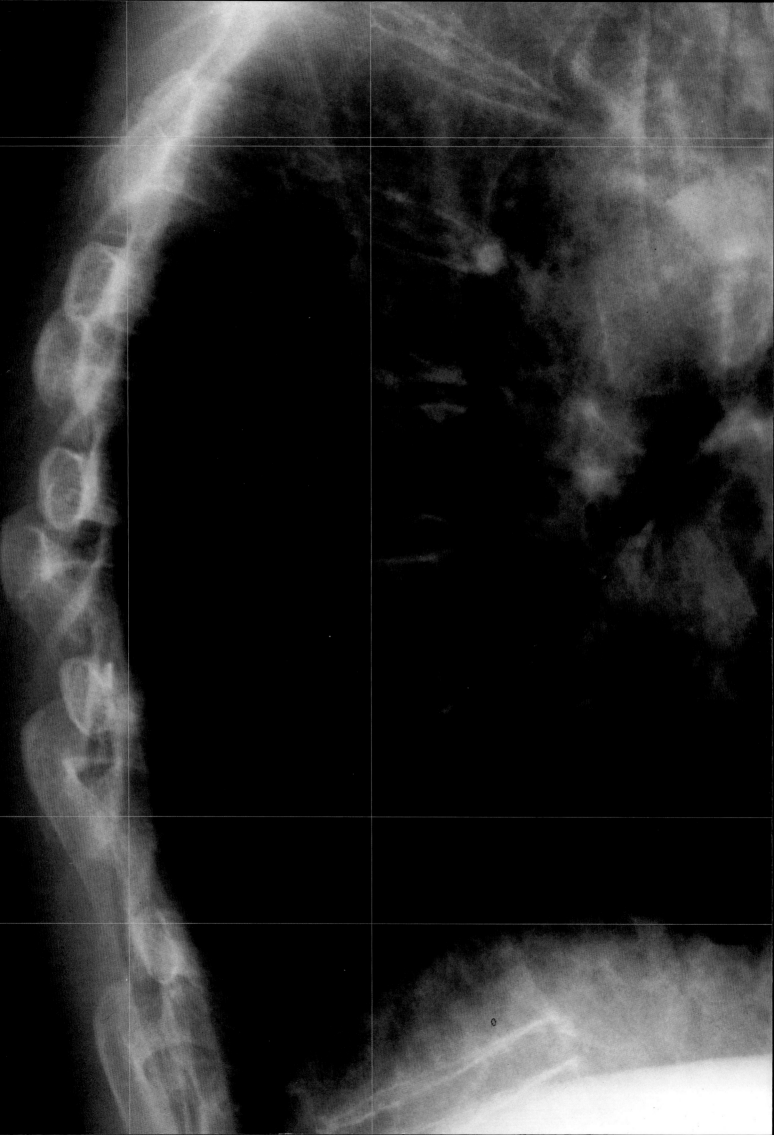

LOVE MISSILE

★ ★ ★ ★ ★

DOMINATOR TRANSCRIPT

NEURAL EQUIPMENT

NATOR

TER

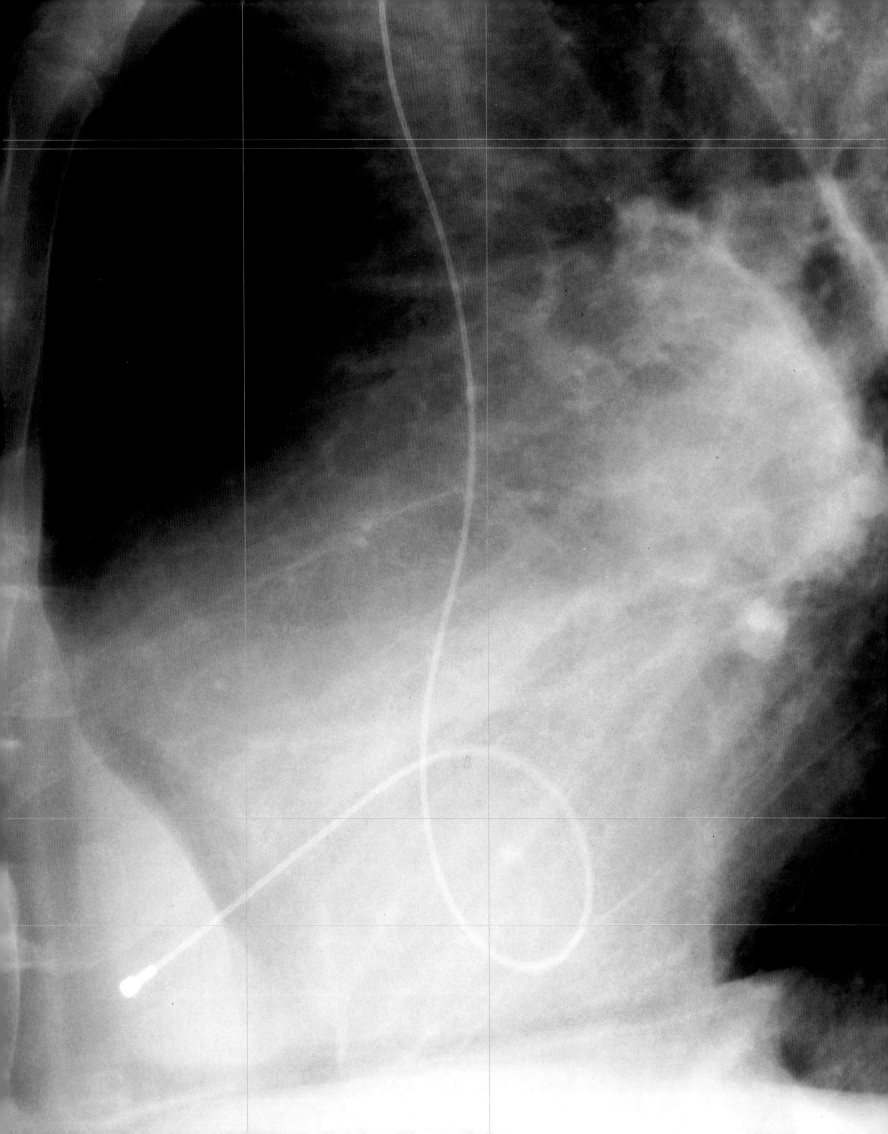

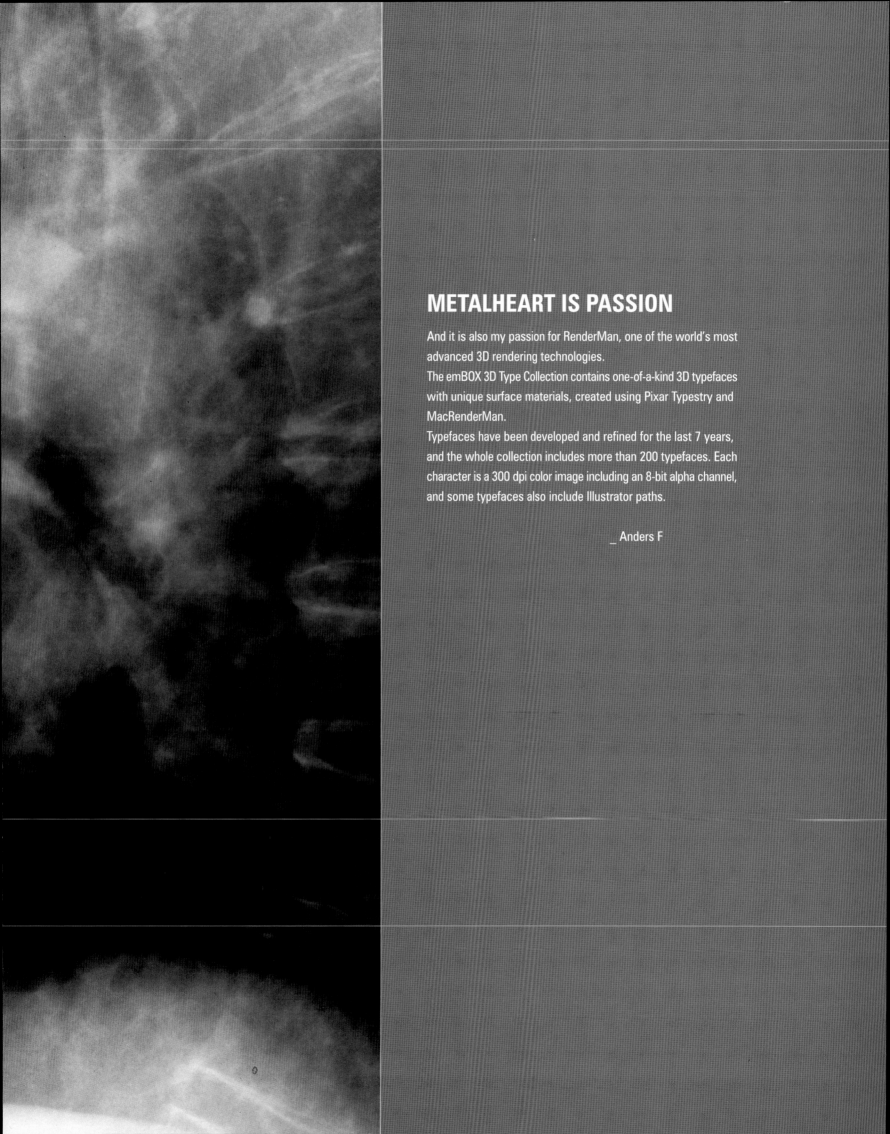

METALHEART IS PASSION

And it is also my passion for RenderMan, one of the world's most
advanced 3D rendering technologies.

The emBOX 3D Type Collection contains one-of-a-kind 3D typefaces
with unique surface materials, created using Pixar Typestry and
MacRenderMan.

Typefaces have been developed and refined for the last 7 years,
and the whole collection includes more than 200 typefaces. Each
character is a 300 dpi color image including an 8-bit alpha channel,
and some typefaces also include Illustrator paths.

_ Anders F

artist/company:	**Anders F Rönnblom,** Studio Matchbox
artwork titles:	RenderMan Type Collection 1, 2, 3 & 4
software used:	Pixar Typestry, Photoshop, Live Picture
comments:	Promotional posters, presented as Giclée Fine Art prints in the Digital Hall of Fame Collection

typefaces displayed: 1. Metal Pizza 2. Cyber Smoke 3. Heavy Bronze 4. Freaky Nuclear 5. Pontille Plate 6. Cyber Joker 7. Cyber Sprouts 8. Decoder Plant 9. Gilles Modi 10. Convalian Sheet 11. Soft Shells 12. Chantarelle Crack (Cracked Beauty) 13. Freaky Plaster 14. Cyber Ribbons (Mellow Ribbons) 15. Cyber Silk 16. Freaky Silver

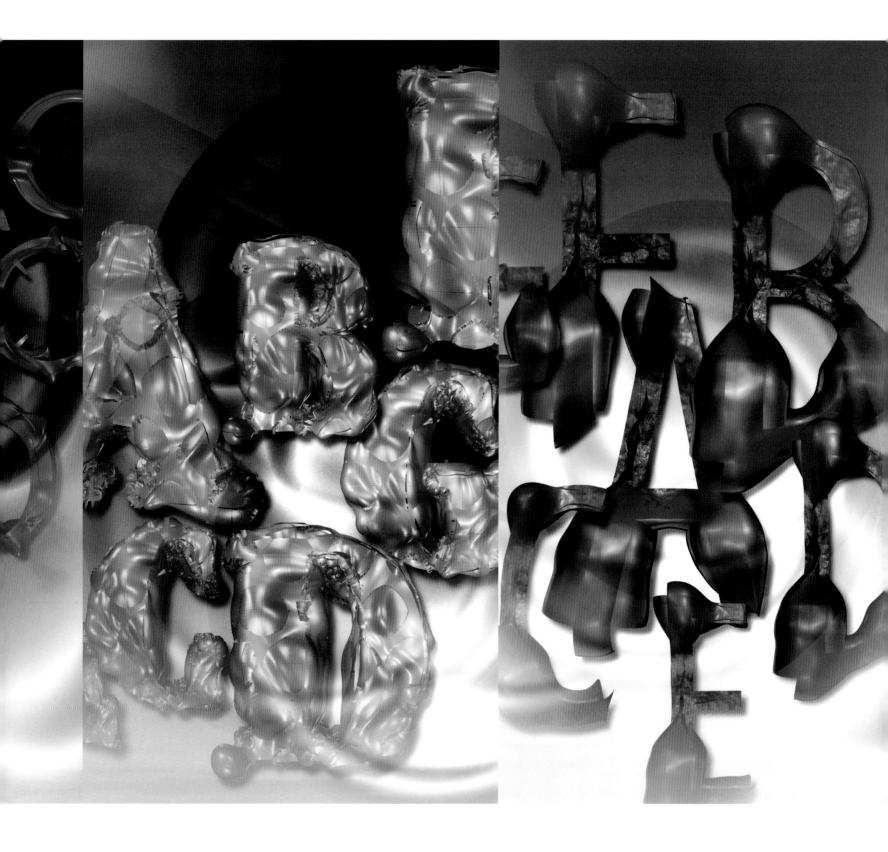

typeface displayed: **emBOX Justinelle Bronze** typeface displayed: **emBOX Caledonia Bronze** typeface displayed: **emBOX Old Metal**

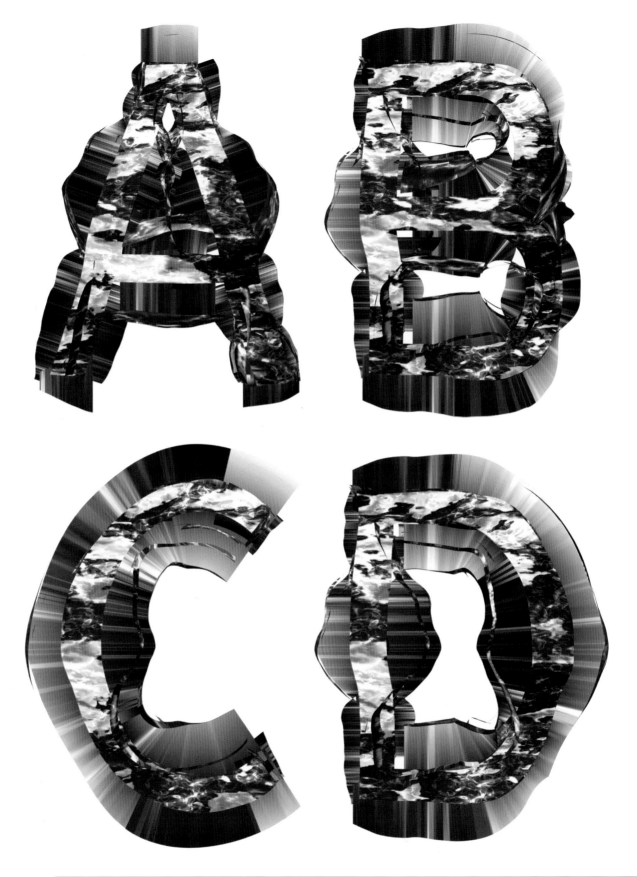

emBOX Freaky Water 3 (Cyber Ocean)

artist/company:	**Anders F Rönnblom,** Studio Matchbox	software used:	Pixar Typestry, Photoshop, Live Picture
artworktitle:	emBOX Typeface samples from the years 1993-2000	comments:	Cyber Ocean rocks

emBOX Freaky Floofy Circus

emBOX Magician's Mask

emBOX Freaky Floofy Bronze

emBOX Cybereem

emBOX Freaky Water 1

emBOX Psycho Root

emBOX Freaky Water 2

emBOX Cyber Ribbon 2

emBOX Cyber Lizard 1

emBOX Freaky Bronze

emBOX Cyber Swirl

emBOX Cyber Juker

emBOX Swirl Ribbons

emBOX Half-Cracked Beauty

comments: Selected files available on the complementary MetalHeart CD

artist/company:	**Anders F Rönnblom,** Studio Matchbox	software used: Pixar Typestry, Photoshop
artwork title:	emBOX Soft Paradiso	comments: Transparent

artwork title: Tribute to Gianni Versace

comments: 3D type based on the font Scratched Out, designed by Pierre di Scullo for the FUSE type library

artist/company:	**Anders F Rönnblom,** Studio Matchbox	software used:	Pixar Typestry, Photoshop, Live Picture
artwork title:	Samples from the emBOX 3D Type collection	comments:	Selected files available on the complementary MetalHeart CD

typefaces displayed: AKZ Metal Supreme, Concrete Supreme, Cyber Ribbons, Floofy Bronze Roman, Weird Wood 13,

Full Smoke Cica, Freaky Nuclear, Corrupt Metal, Cyber Metal Mother

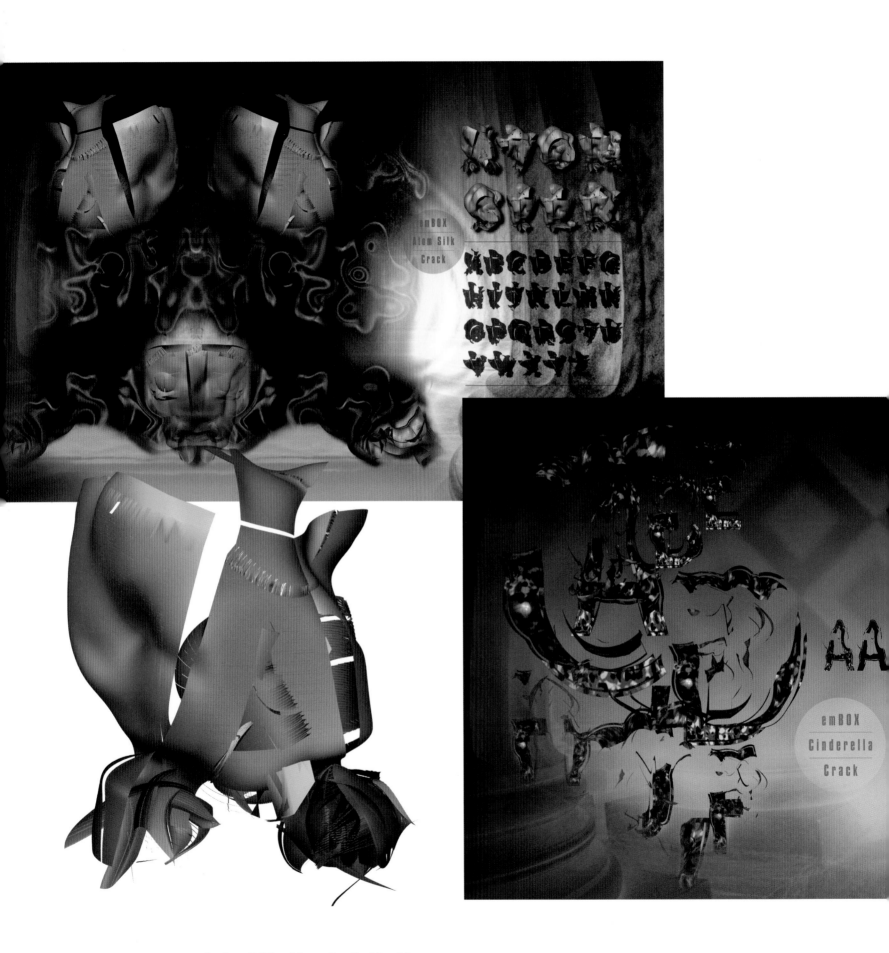

artist/company: **Anders F Rönnblom,** Studio Matchbox

artwork titles: emBOX Atom Silk Crack, emBOX Cinderella Crack, emBOX Pontille Plate

software used: Pixar Typestry, Photoshop, Live Picture

comments: Selected files available on the complementary MetalHeart CD

artist/company: **Anders F Rönnblom,** Studio Matchbox

software used: Pixar Typestry, Photoshop, Live Picture

artwork titles: emBOX Crystopia Deluxe, emBOX Swelled Glass

comments: Crystopia Deluxe based on the Brainreactor Crystopia font

Selected files available on the complementary MetalHeart CD

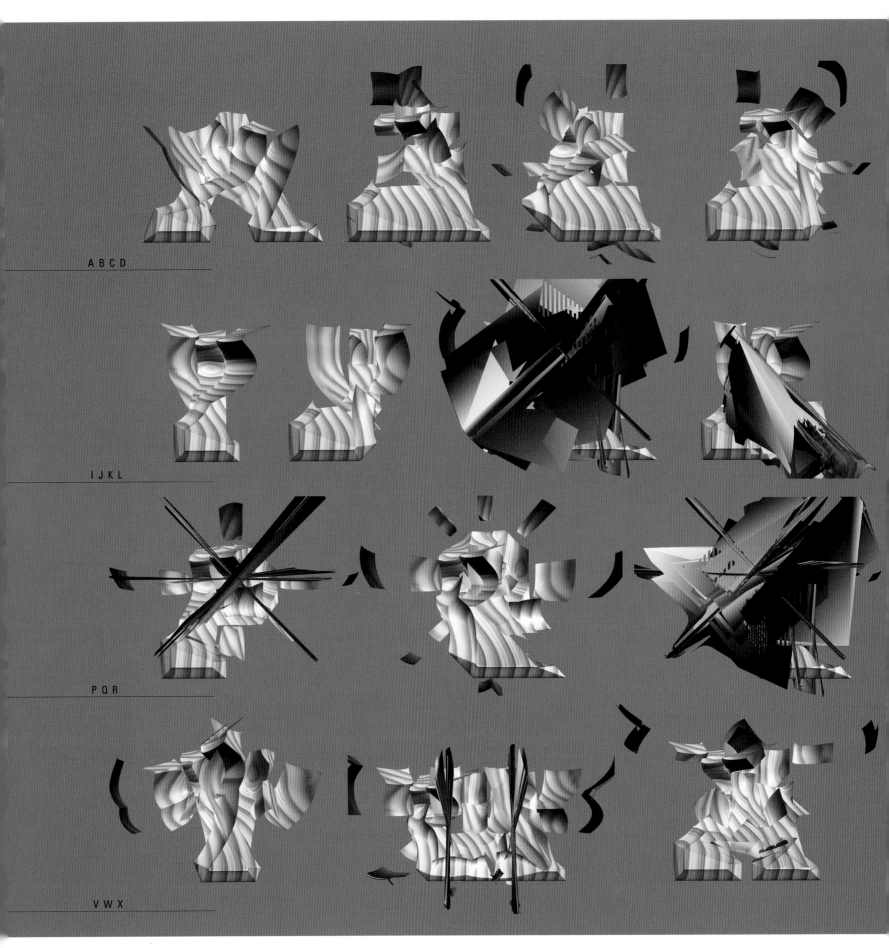

A B C D

I J K L

P Q R

V W X

artist/company: **Anders F Rönnblom,** Studio Matchbox

artwork title: emBOX Extreme Wood

software used: Pixar Typestry, Photoshop, Live Picture

comments: Extreme distortions produced a corrupt typeface

Contents

ANDREAS LINDHOLM is a 29-year old graphic designer from Stockholm, Sweden, who has been designing a great variety of techno display typefaces for the last couple of years. He is also a visual creator and 3D illustrator and has been working with programs such as FreeHand, Photoshop, After Effects and a variety of 3D applications, for both stills, animations and videos. Andreas is currently working as a creative director at Tension Graphics in Stockholm.

Fore_word_06.00

I've been waiting for this book. Three years of personal evolution.

Three years of hard work. Three years of unbeaten positivism.

Still, I've refused hundreds of my own images – artwork that was supposed to have a place in

this collection. Yes, I really wanted to show everything. The work represented in this edition of

MetalHeart (except for some of the typefaces) is not older than three years.

I love my artistry. I love it because I can fully control the process. I love the process of digital art.

I love abstract things: shapes, shadows and colors.

Wherever you are, you are always surrounded by beautiful and inspiring details.

On a recent domestic flight, for example, I looked amazingly at a small area on the aircraft's wing.

It had a very nice construction with hundreds of tiny nits and aggressively shaped aluminum

plates. Reflections from the blue sky made the image complete,

and later it inspired me to create a piece that can be found in this book.

MetalHeart is made with passion for this kind of illustrative and experimental work.

MetalHeart is love.

_Andreas Lindholm

Fore_word_07.00

MetalHeart is the description of a process, not of a result.

That's why it has taken three years to complete.

It has been an ongoing process of taking new and giant leaps with the current technology,

and falling deep into the realm of pure digital art and design. And, to be honest, the majority of art

in this book couldn't have been successfully created without the aid of today's digital software.

My passion for digital design is based on the power of the pixel. The power of noise and fractals.

The power of layers and channels. And the power of using blending calculations.

It is also the power of RenderMan – were it not for that technology, I would have been nowhere.

My passion for this process has been growing through the last ten years, and so has my network

– a great community of artists all around the world. It is therefore a great pleasure to see the

powerful contributions to the Guest Artist Gallery.

The new way of designing things. The new way of expressing.

It's art that matters. Art is important.

MetalHeart is art.

_Anders F Rönnblom

ANDERS F RÖNNBLOM is a 54-year old art director and musician from Stockholm, Sweden, who has been running his own design firm, Studio Matchbox, for more than 25 years. Together with photographer Mariann Eklund, he publishes the exclusive magazine EFX Art & Design, and he is also the curator of the Digital Hall of Fame art exhibition. Anders F has for many years been designing experimental 3D typefaces using RenderMan technology, and is also a dedicated Live Picture user.

Some of fonts and typefaces included on the emBOX/Brainreactor Prototype CD.

The METALHEART book project started in 1998 with the emBOX/Brainreactor Prototype CD, containing fonts and 3D typefaces that were sent out to digital designers for digital experimenting. We wanted them to use and abuse our alphabets, and then send us their artworks. Our plan was to publish a book of new experimental digital design. However, it took us quite some time to complete this book, because we didn't actually know what was going to be in there. We didn't have a clue of what kinds of images people would send to us, and in the beginning we didn't even know too well what to include ourselves. Initially we received a few files from people who had used the fonts and typefaces for flyers and logowork (see opposite page), but it wasn't until we published Andreas' spectacular graphics in EFX Art & Design magazine, that we started to see a new attitude grow among digital designers. And it spread over the Internet. Andreas published new fonts. People started to talk about MetalHeart. And we received more and more interesting files. We also invited many renowned digital artists to participate. For the past three years, we have seen the development of a new graphic style, a new exciting graphic language among today's young digital designers.

The METALHEART book is a document of this digital development. The book is an exclusive collection of contemporary digital design and typographic experiments, and it features a guest gallery of more than 30 international digital artists presenting illustrations, flyers, posters, CD covers, web design, and lots of self promotional graphics.

Welcome to METALHEART.

_The authors

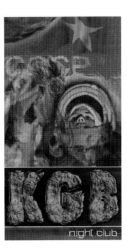

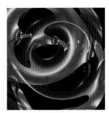

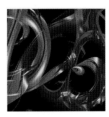

Designed by: **Dave Taylor,** USA, using a modified version of Andreas' Decoder font.

Designed by: **Lionel Barat,** France, using Anders F's Freaky Plaster typeface.

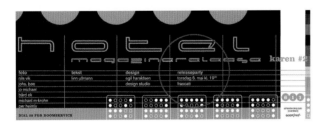

Designed by: **Aaron Spesard,** USA, using a modified version of Andreas' Octane font.

Designed by: **Filippo Spiezia,** Italy, using Anders F's Cyber Bronze typeface.

Designed by: **Egil Haraldsen,** Norway, using Andreas' Neutronica font.

Designed by: **Filippo Spiezia,** Italy, using Andreas' Crystopia font.

Designed by: **Jeff Valdor,** USA, using Anders F's Cyber Joker typeface.

Designed by: **Bruce Palmer,** USA, using Andreas' Intergalactic font.

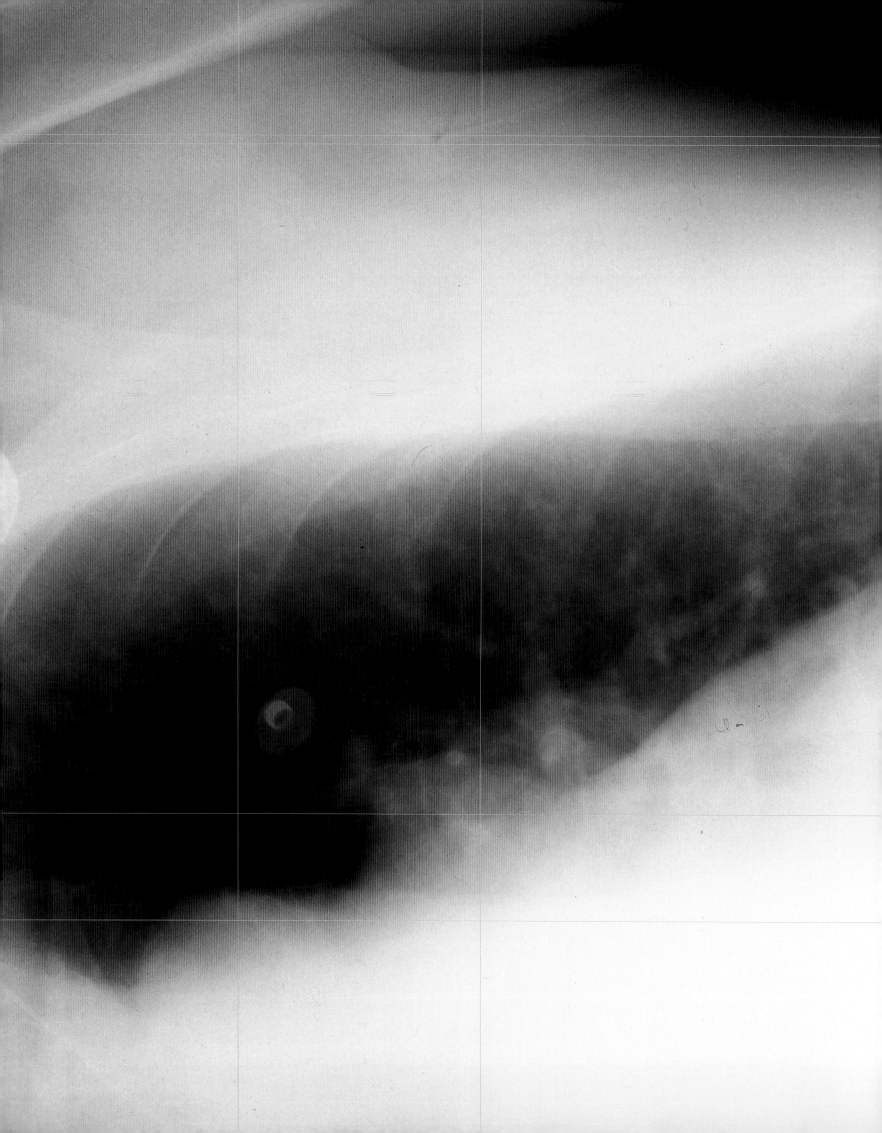

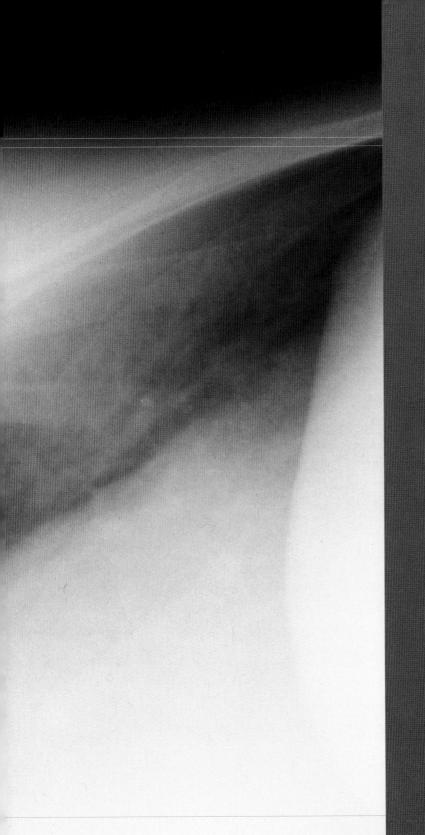

METALHEART IS PLEASURE

There are thousands of them. Thousands of beautifully designed typefaces out there. Handcrafted, perfect and readable for all kinds of written text.

Brainreactor fonts are something else. Not always readable, very rarely made by hand, and far from perfect. Some people like them, some people don't.

Brainreactor fonts are prototypes for the future, my future. Concepts, ideas and elaborations with the printed word in mind made this collection. A collection of fonts that was never meant to be released for the public. Now they are, and people around the world are using them every day for all kinds of designwork.

I started with these elaborations in 1995, and until today I've created approximately 200 different full alphabetical setups for my own pleasure. About 20 of them are represented on the MetalHeart CD in the back of this book. Others will be released in the future.

Use them as you like.

Maybe new ideas will be born.

Brainreactor fonts are pleasure.

_Andreas

PRENOPTICA
Built for speed

PRENOPTICA
ABCDEFGHIJKLMNOPQRSTUVWXYZ
1234567890

VACCU-BOMB
Do not inhale

VACCU-BOMB
ABCDEFGHIJKLMNOPQRSTUVWXYZ
1234567890

CRYSTOPIA
Candystore on Mars

crystopia
abcdefghijklmnopqrstuvwxyz

ULTIMATE SURVIVAL
399 days in the Gobi Desert

ULTIMATE SURVIVAL
ABCDEFGHIJKLMNOPQRSTUVWXYZ
1234567890

DECODER
Future in the past

DECODER
abcdefghijklmnopqrstuvwxyz
1234567890

OCTANE
Drunk by petrolium

Octane
abcdefghijklmnopqrstuvwxyz
1234567890

NEUTRONICA
Tiny tiny moe

NEUTRONICA
ABCDEFGHIJKLMNOPQRSTUVWXYZ
1234567890

VIRUS
Ebola and Microsoft

VIRUS
abcdefghijklmnopqrstuvwxyz
1234567890

REACTIVATOR
Please, use it for real

REACTIVATOR
abcdefghijklmnopqrstuvwxyz
1234567890

BUMBLEBEE
Some cool words

bumblebee
abcdefghijklmnopqrstuvwxyz

artist/company: **Andreas Lindholm,** Brainreactor, Sweden

artwork title: Various fonts from the Brainreactor collection

software used: FreeHand, Fontographer

comments: www.abstructure.com

PROLOGIC
Bobby Surround

PROLOGIC

abcdefghijklmnopqrstuvwxyz
1234567890

CALCULATOR
The most ugly in the world

calculator

abcdefghijklmnopqrstuvwxyz
1234567890

FUTUREMARK
There is something

futuremark

abcdefghijklmnopqrstuvwxyz
1234567890

NEODREAMS
The 'Rs' are rare

NEODREAMS

ABCDEFGHIJKLMNOPQRSTUVWXYZ
1234567890

MF PROPAGANDA
Sorry, not to be released

MF PROPAGANDA

ABCDEFGHIJKLMNOPQRSTUVWXYZ
1234567890

399 MISSILE
Scumbag Scud

399 MISSILE

ABCDEFGHIJKLMNOPQRSTUVWXYZ
1234567890

INTERGALACTIC
StarTrek will continue

INTERGALACTIC

ABCDEFGHIJKLMNOPQRSTUVWXYZ
1234567890

AMRAAM
A Medium Range Air-to-Air missile

AMRAAM

ABCDEFGHIJKLMNOPQRSTUVWXYZ
1234567890

ELASTICA
Minimal hardcore

ELASTICA

ABCDEFGHIJKLMNOPQRSTUVWXYZ
1234567890

INDUSTRIAL FAITH
Kom fram ur mörkret

INDUSTRIAL FAITH

ABCDEFGHIJKLMNOPQRSTUVWXYZ
1234567890

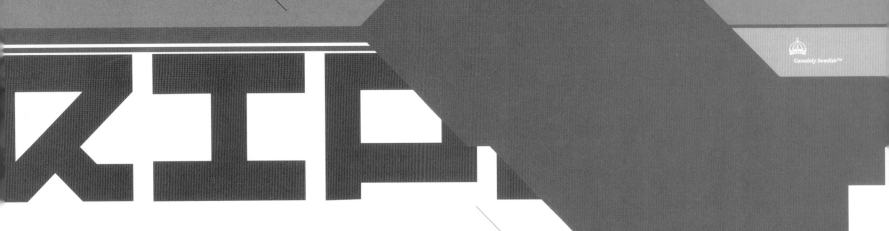

RIP

RIPOFF-STYLE
0449

abcdefghijklmnopqrstuvwxyz
1234567890 moon2mars.com

abcdefghijklmnopqrstuvwxyz
1234567890 moon2mars.com

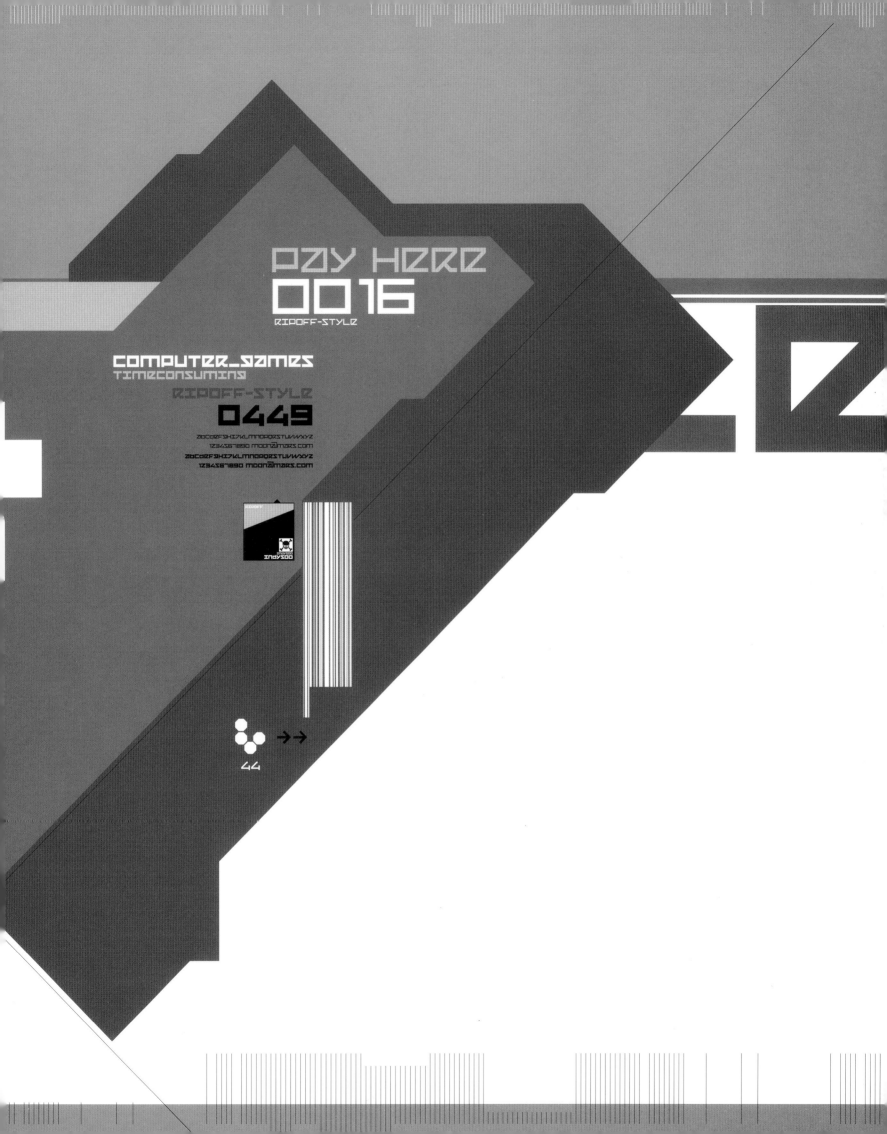

PAY HERE
0016
RIPOFF-STYLE

computer_games
timeconsuming

RIPOFF-STYLE
0449

abcdefghijklmnopqrstuvwxyz
1234567890 moon2mars.com
abcdefghijklmnopqrstuvwxyz
1234567890 moon2mars.com

44

abcdefghijklmnopqrstuvwxyz 1234567890
ABCDEFGHIJKLMNOPQRSTUVWXYZ 1234567890

ABCDEFGHIJKLMNOPQRSTUVWXYZ 1234567890
abcdefghijklmnopqrstuvwxyz 1234567890

ABCDEFGHIJKLMNOPQRSTUVWXYZ 1234567890
abcdefghijklmnopqrstuvwxyz 1234567890

artist/company: **Andreas Lindholm,** Brainreactor

artwork title: Dominator Font

software used: FreeHand, Fontographer

comments: www.abstructure.com

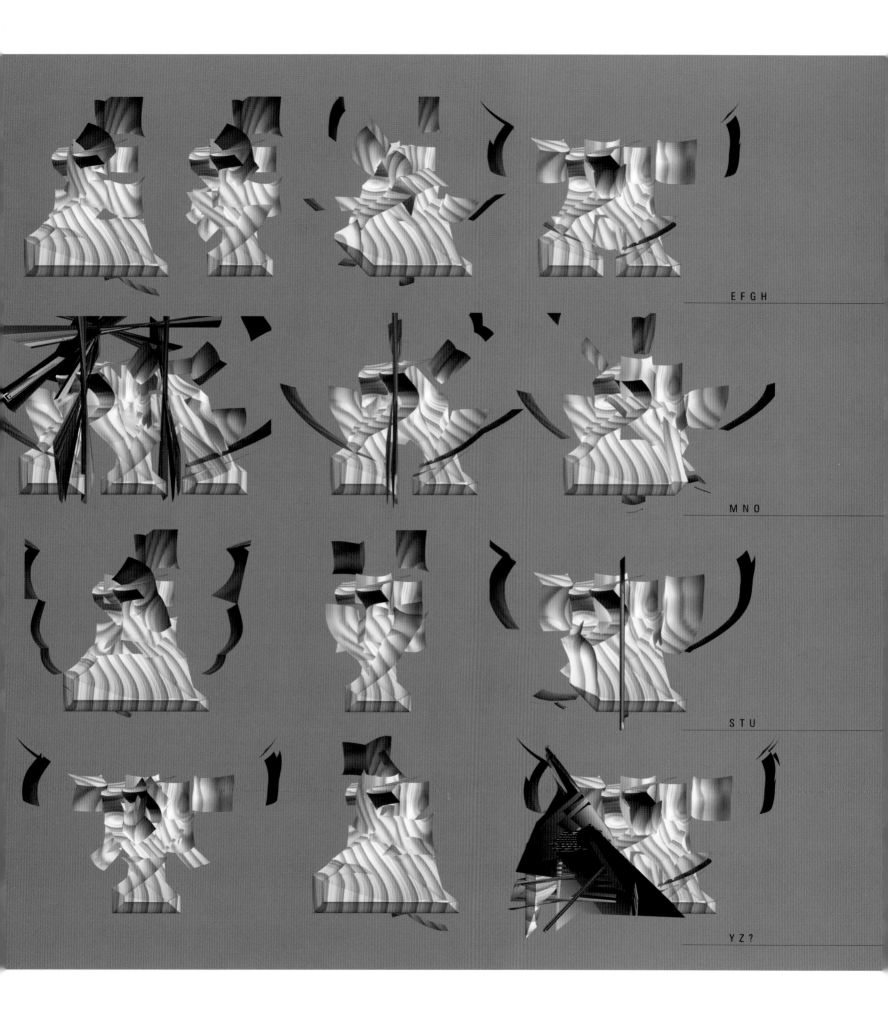

EFGH

MNO

STU

YZ?

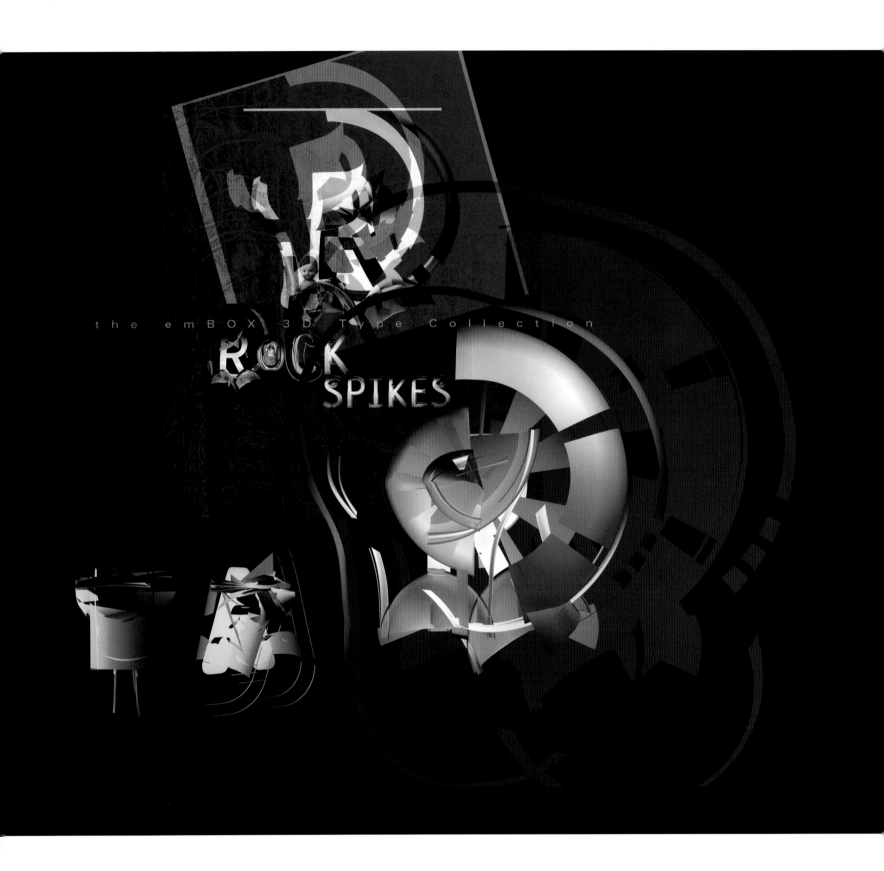

artist/company:	**Anders F Rönnblom,** Studio Matchbox	software used:	Pixar Typestry, Photoshop, Live Picture
artwork title:	emBOX Rock Spikes	comments:	emBOX catalog spread

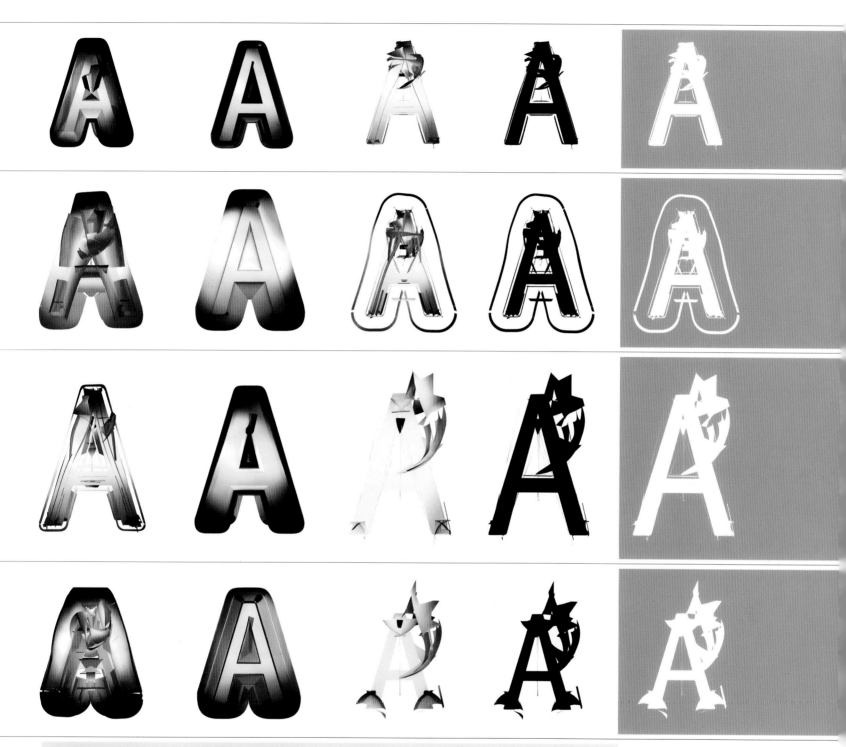

THE emBOX ROCK RELIEF MATERIAL IS A STONE-LIKE SURFACE THAT HAS HAD ITS SPOTS WORN AWAY. IT IS BUILT AROUND A GENERAL PURPOSE MATERIAL THAT ALLOWS YOU TO CONTROL COLOR, SHININESS, METALNESS, TRANSPARENCY AND GLOW, TOGETHER WITH A RELIEF THAT PRODUCES A FRACTAL SURFACE. THE MAXIMUM HEIGHT, THE ROUGHNESS AND THE RUGGEDNESS OF THE RELIEF CAN BE CONTROLLED FOR EROSION EFFECTS, AND THE DISPLACEMENT PARAMETER IS USED FOR EXTREME DISTORTION EFFECTS. A WELL-BALANCED MIX BETWEEN THESE VALUES WILL PRODUCE A WIDE VARIETY OF BOTH SMOOTH AND SPIKY SURFACE MATERIALS.

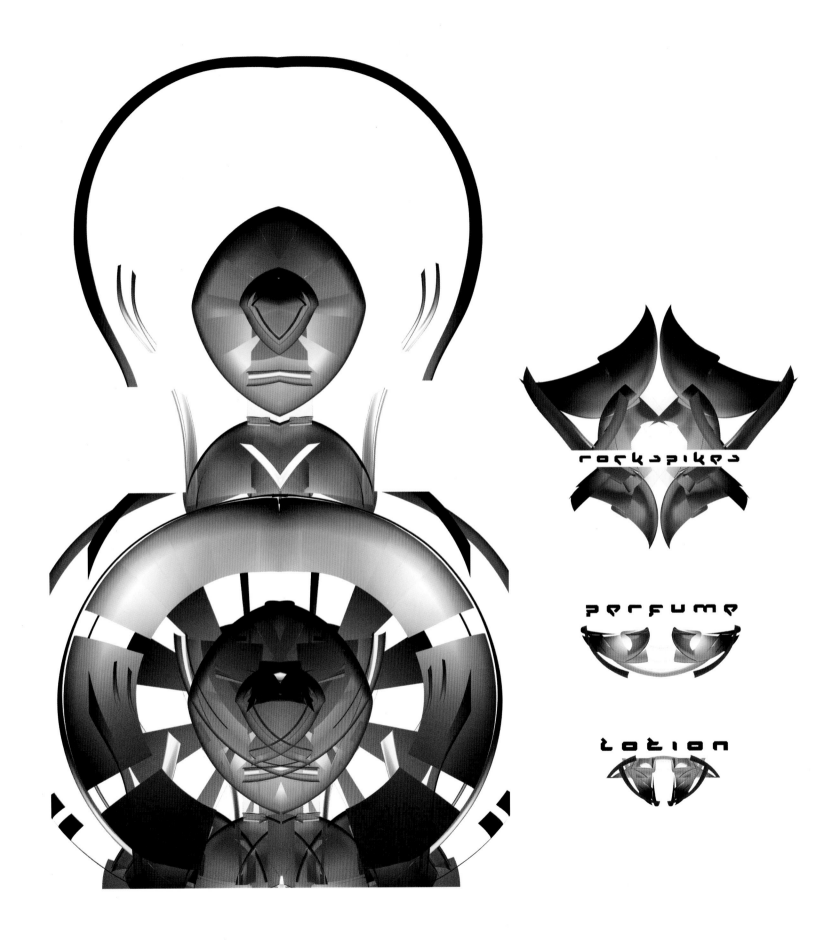

artist/company:	**Anders F Rönnblom,** Studio Matchbox		software used:	Pixar Typestry, Photoshop
artwork titles:	RenderMan sculpture 1 & 2, Labels 1, 2 & 3		typeface used:	emBOX Rock Spikes and Brainreactor Futuremark

comments: Sketches for cosmetic products

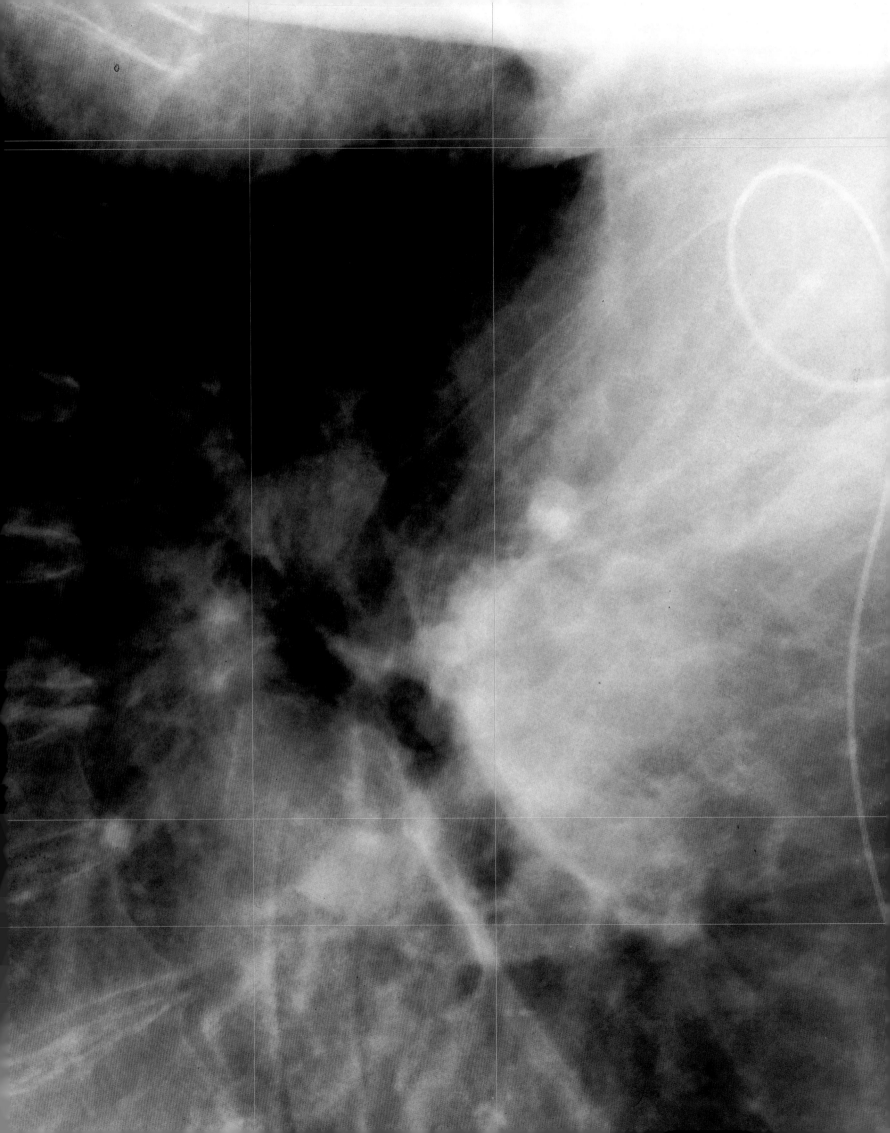

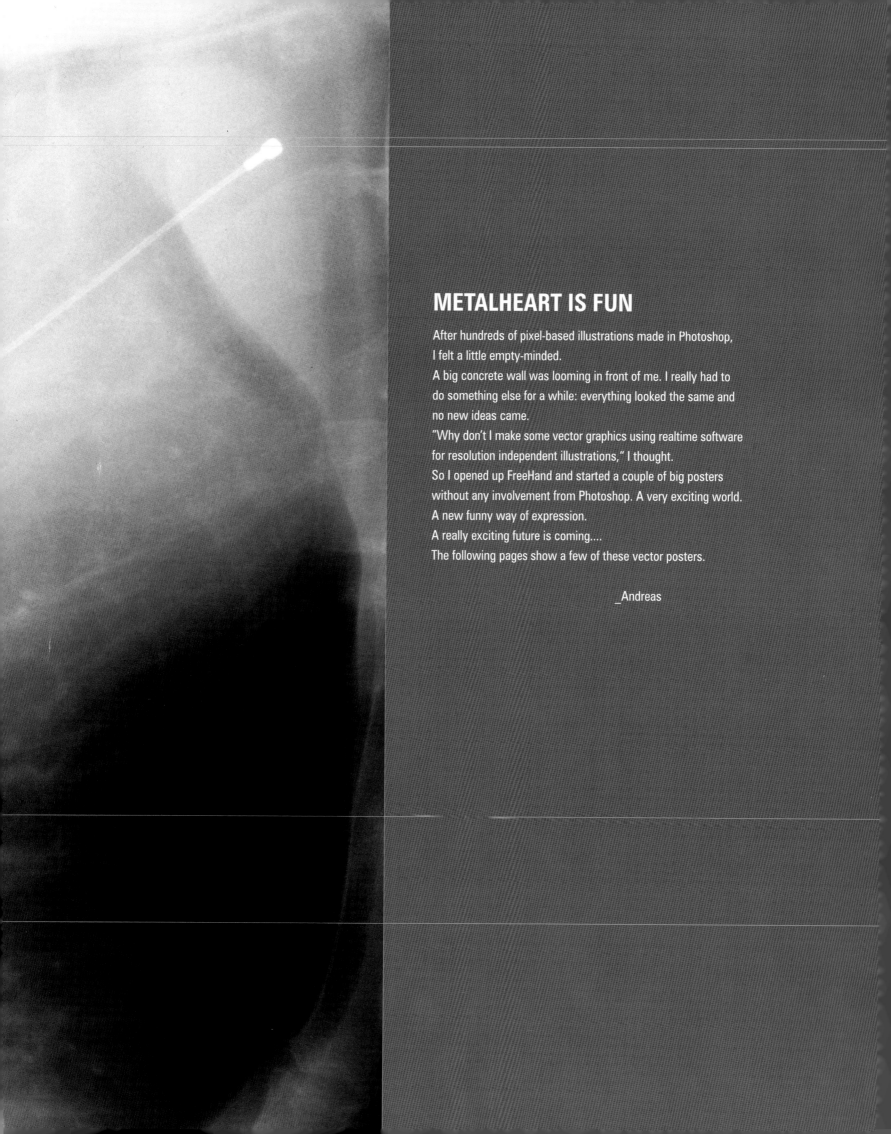

METALHEART IS FUN

After hundreds of pixel-based illustrations made in Photoshop,
I felt a little empty-minded.
A big concrete wall was looming in front of me. I really had to
do something else for a while: everything looked the same and
no new ideas came.
"Why don't I make some vector graphics using realtime software
for resolution independent illustrations," I thought.
So I opened up FreeHand and started a couple of big posters
without any involvement from Photoshop. A very exciting world.
A new funny way of expression.
A really exciting future is coming....
The following pages show a few of these vector posters.

_Andreas

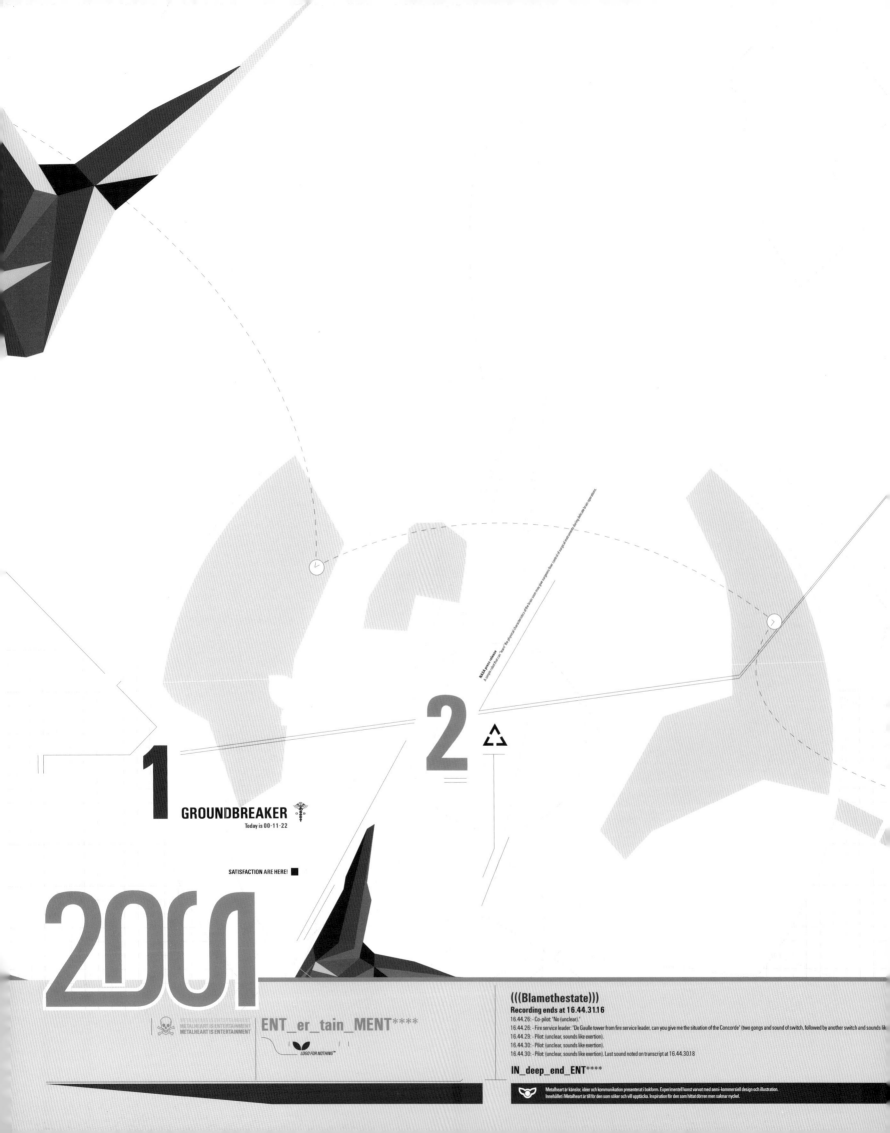

1

GROUNDBREAKER ⚕

Today is 00-11-22

SATISFACTION ARE HERE! ■

2001

💀 METALHEART IS ENTERTAINMENT
METALHEART IS ENTERTAINMENT

ENT_er_tain_MENT****

🌱 *LOGO FOR NOTHING™*

2 △

(((Blamethestate)))
Recording ends at 16.44.31.16
16.44.26: - Co-pilot: "No (unclear)."
16.44.26: - Fire service leader: "De Gaulle tower from fire service leader, can you give me the situation of the Concorde" (two gongs and sound of switch, followed by another switch and sounds lik
16.44.29: - Pilot: (unclear, sounds like exertion).
16.44.30: - Pilot: (unclear, sounds like exertion).
16.44.30: - Pilot: (unclear, sounds like exertion). Last sound noted on transcript at 16.44.30.18

IN_deep_end_ENT**

👁 Metalheart är känslor, idéer och kommunikation presenterat i bokform. Experimentell konst varvat med semi-kommersiell design och illustration.
Innehållet i Metalheart är till för den som söker och vill upptäcka. Inspiration för den som hittat dörren men saknar nyckel.

LOVE DESIGN

METALHEART IS ENTERTAINMENT
VER_sion_ONE_point_O

http://

METALHEART IS LOVE

2000-11-22

DELICIOUS
DELERIOUS
DELETED
DESTRUCTED

DELICIOUS
DELERIOUS
DELETED
DESTRUCTED

DENTISTRY

ACTION DENTAL SURGERY
AC_tion_MEN_tal_SURGERY

METALHEART****

700x1000 mm Poster

Genuinly Swedish™

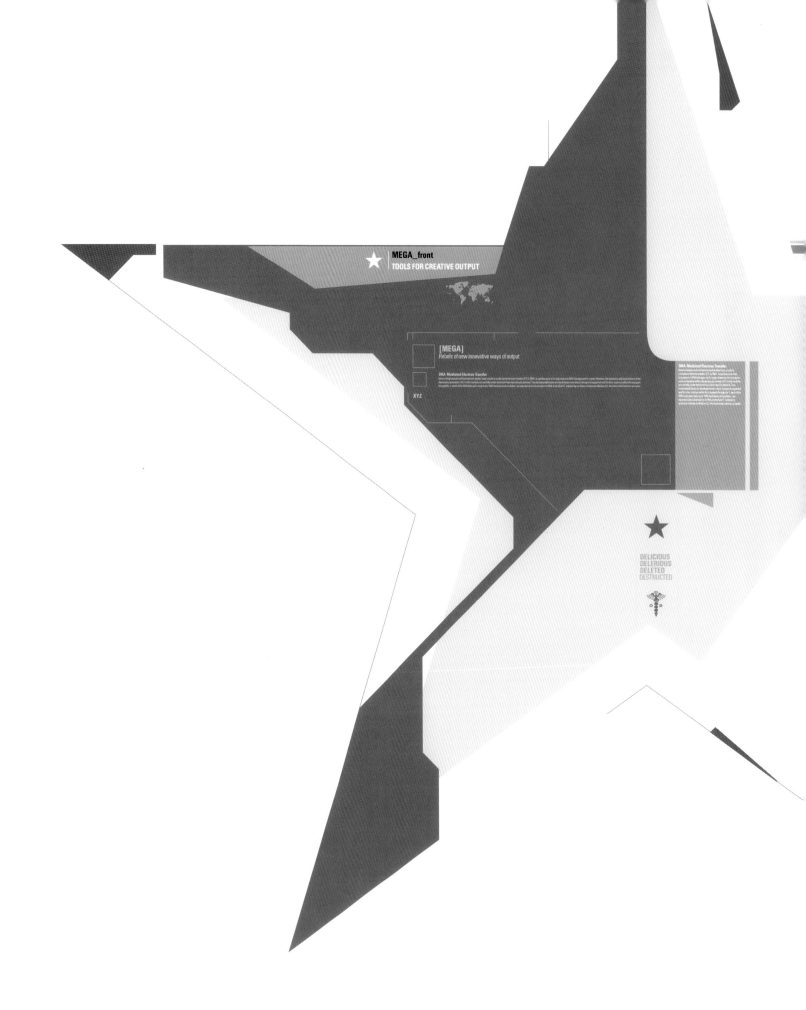

artist/company: **Andreas Lindholm,** Tension Graphics

software used: FreeHand

artwork title: Megafont Illustration for 2001 calender

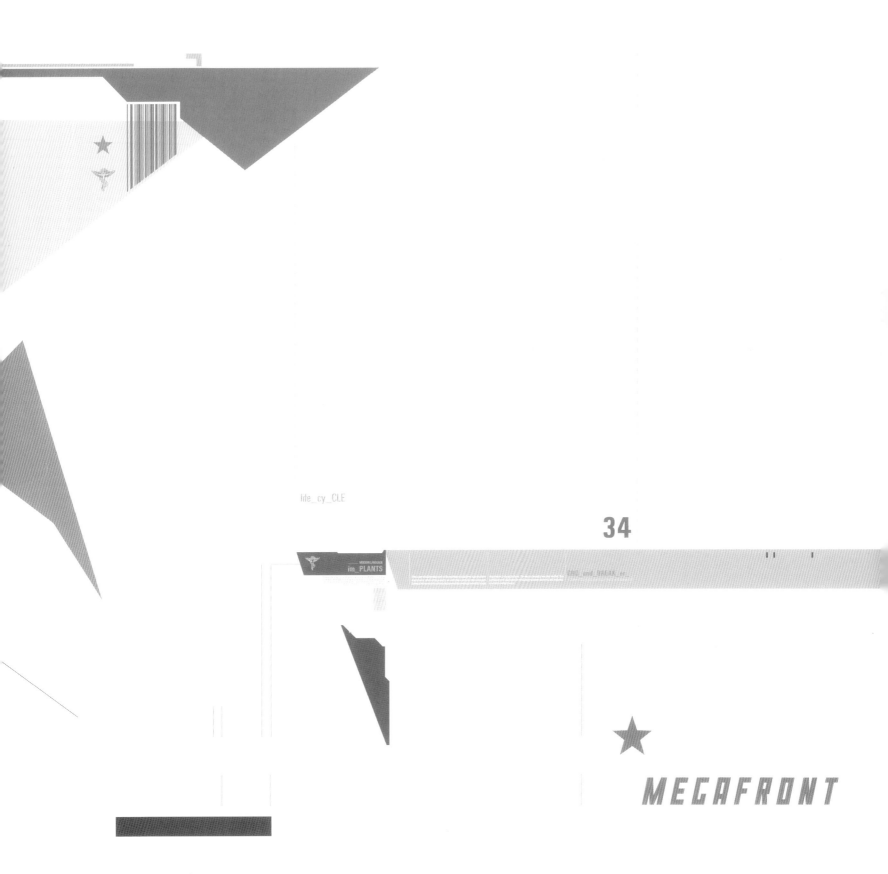

life_cy_CLE

34

im_PLANTS

MEGAFRONT

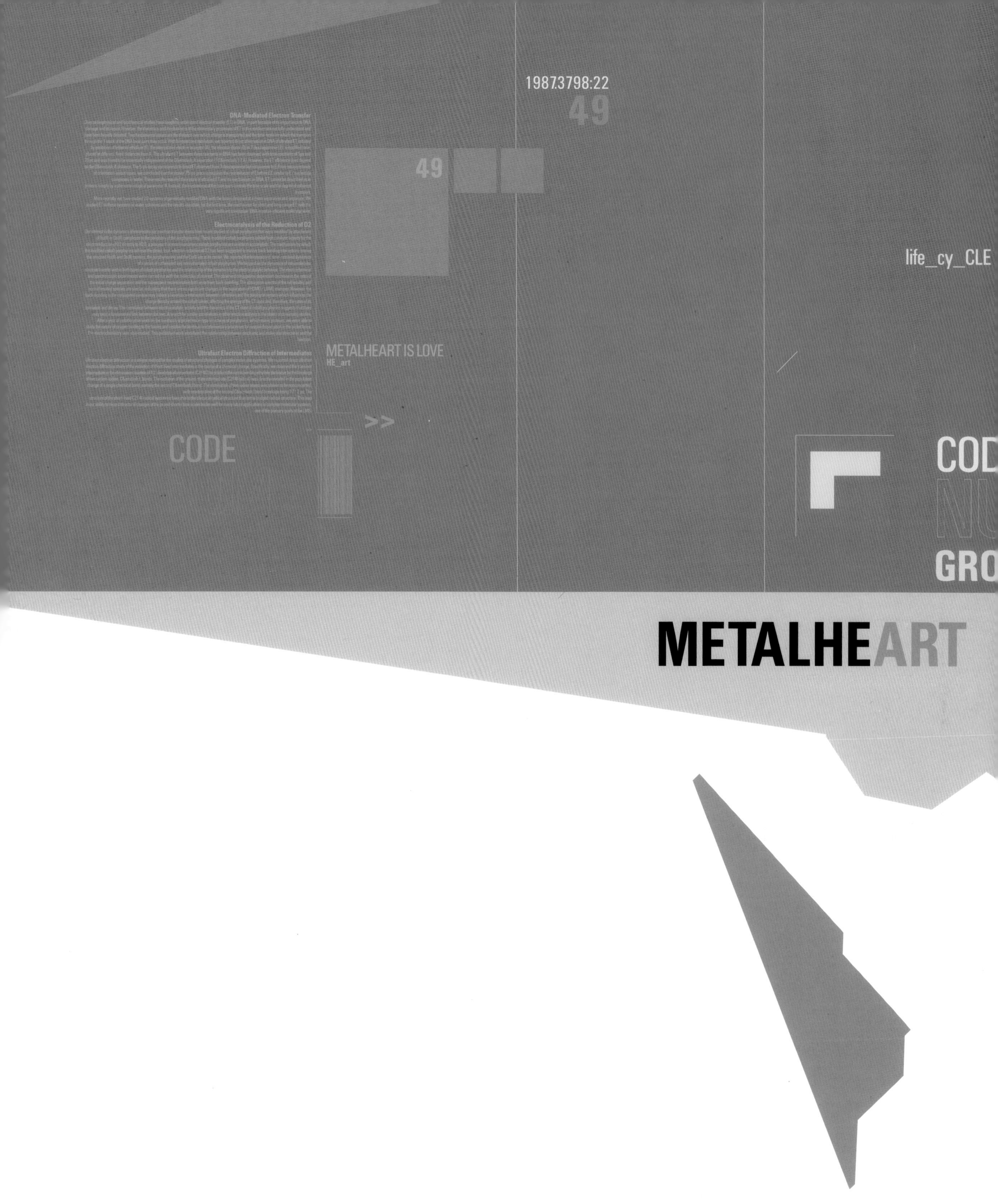
DNA-Mediated Electron Transfer
Electrocatalysis of the Reduction of O2
Ultrafast Electron Diffraction of Intermediates
49
METALHEART IS LOVE
HE_art
>>
CODE
1987.3798:22
49
life_cy_CLE
COD
GRO
METALHEART

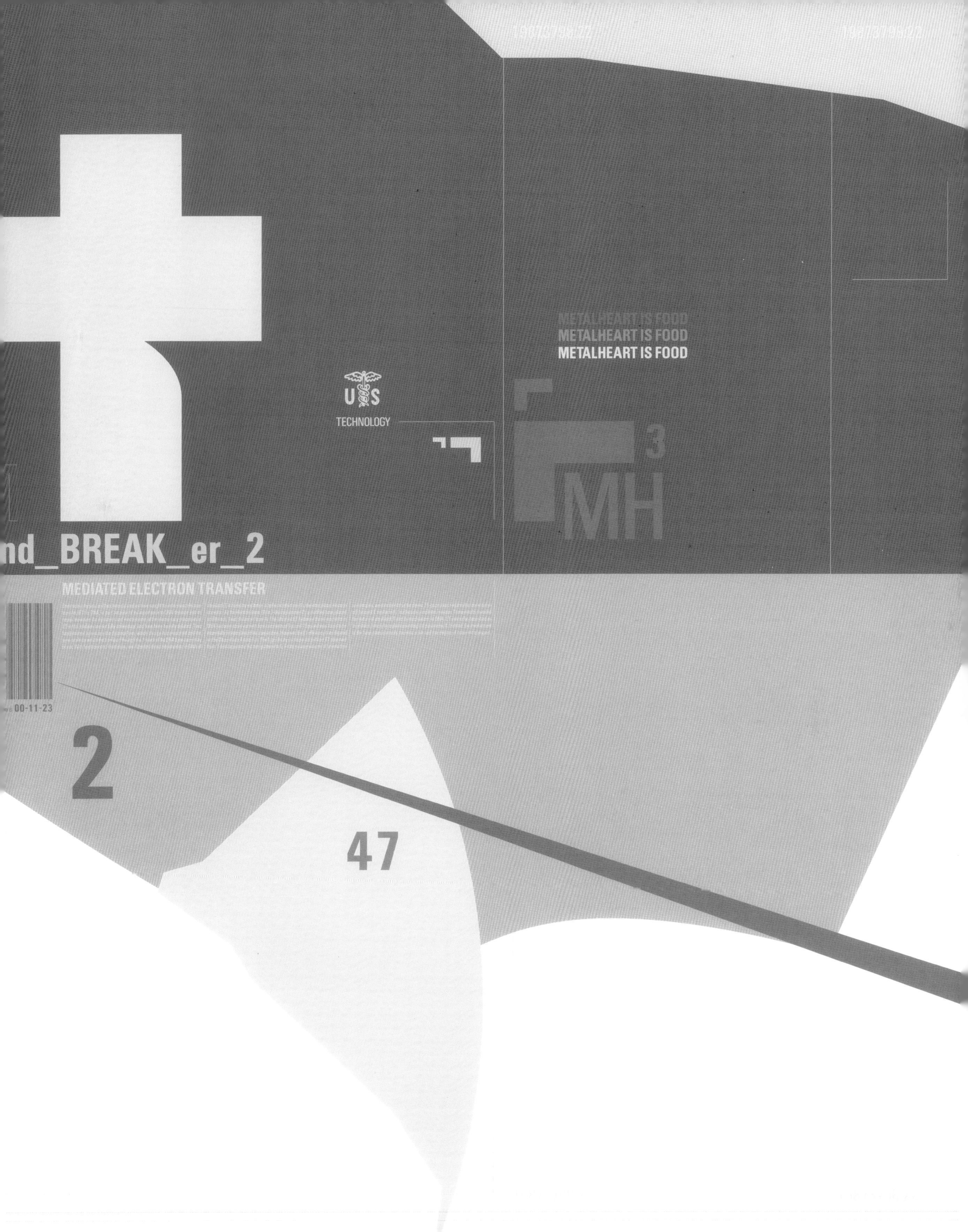

nd_BREAK_er_2

MEDIATED ELECTRON TRANSFER

TECHNOLOGY

U S

METALHEART IS FOOD
METALHEART IS FOOD
METALHEART IS FOOD

MH³

00-11-23

2

47

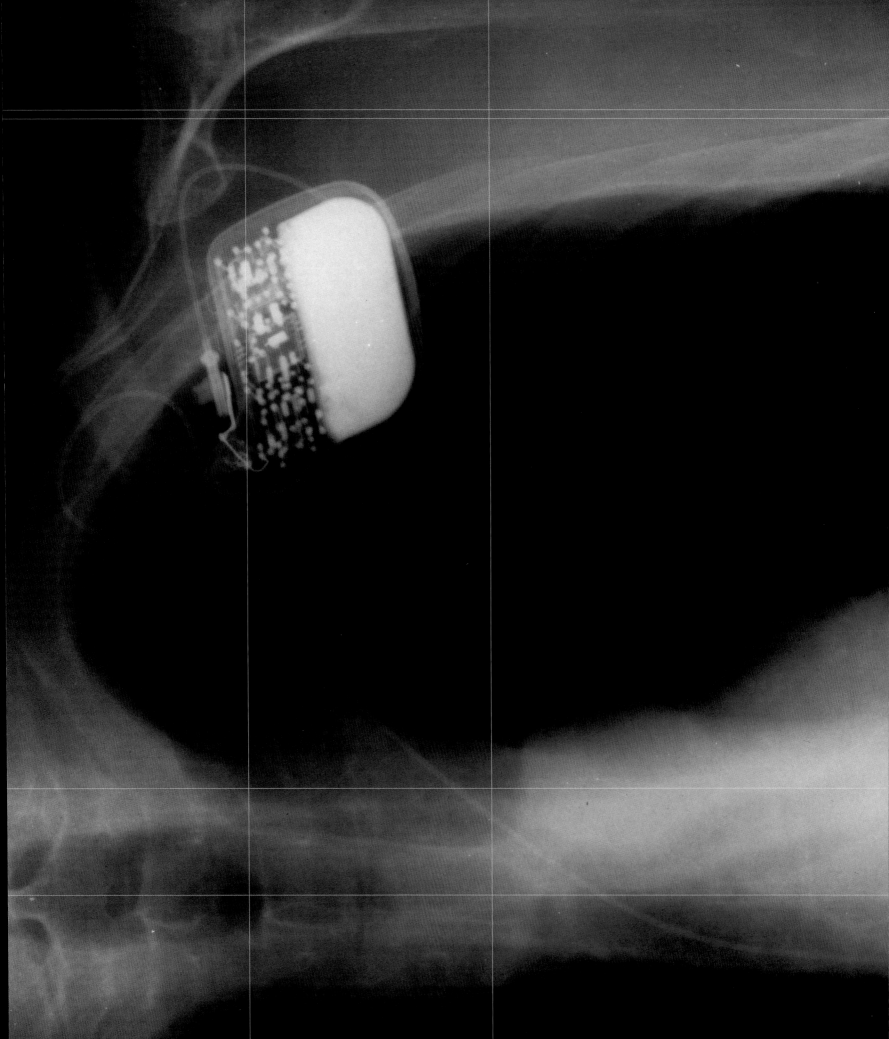

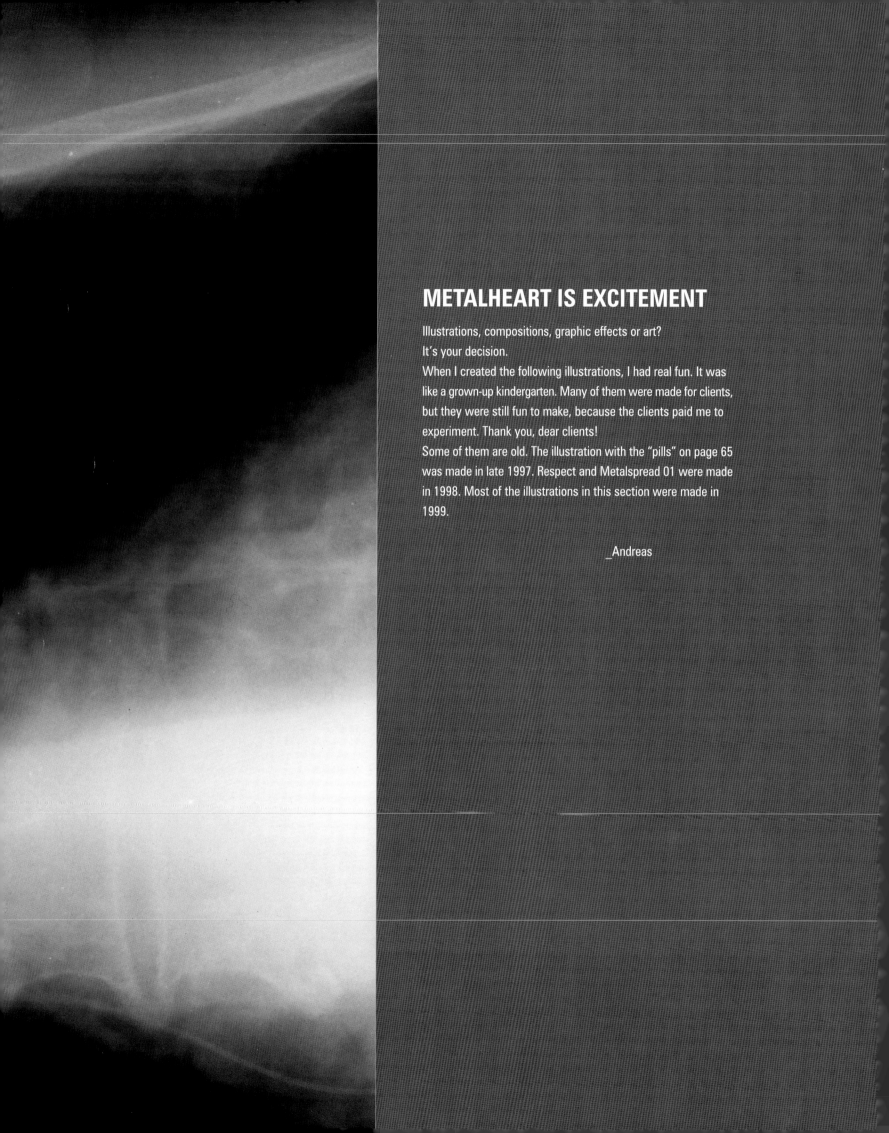

METALHEART IS EXCITEMENT

Illustrations, compositions, graphic effects or art?
It's your decision.
When I created the following illustrations, I had real fun. It was
like a grown-up kindergarten. Many of them were made for clients,
but they were still fun to make, because the clients paid me to
experiment. Thank you, dear clients!
Some of them are old. The illustration with the "pills" on page 65
was made in late 1997. Respect and Metalspread 01 were made
in 1998. Most of the illustrations in this section were made in
1999.

_Andreas

artist/company: **Andreas Lindholm,** Brainreactor

software used: Photoshop, FreeHand

artwork title: Burnback

"So, at your convenience, you have priority to land."
"Gear."
o" (two switch noises).

artist/company:	**Andreas Lindholm,** Brainreactor	software used:	Photoshop, FreeHand, Maya
artwork title:	Developmental Remix	comments:	Just another remix

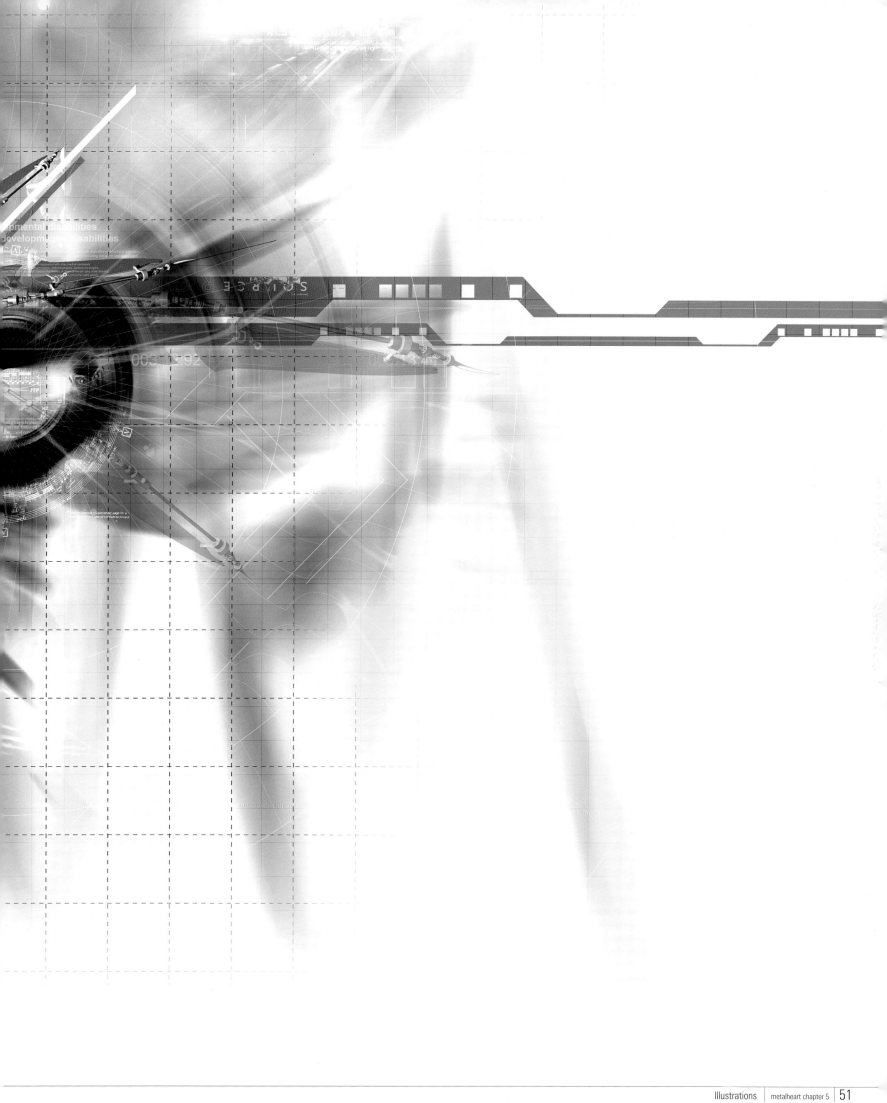

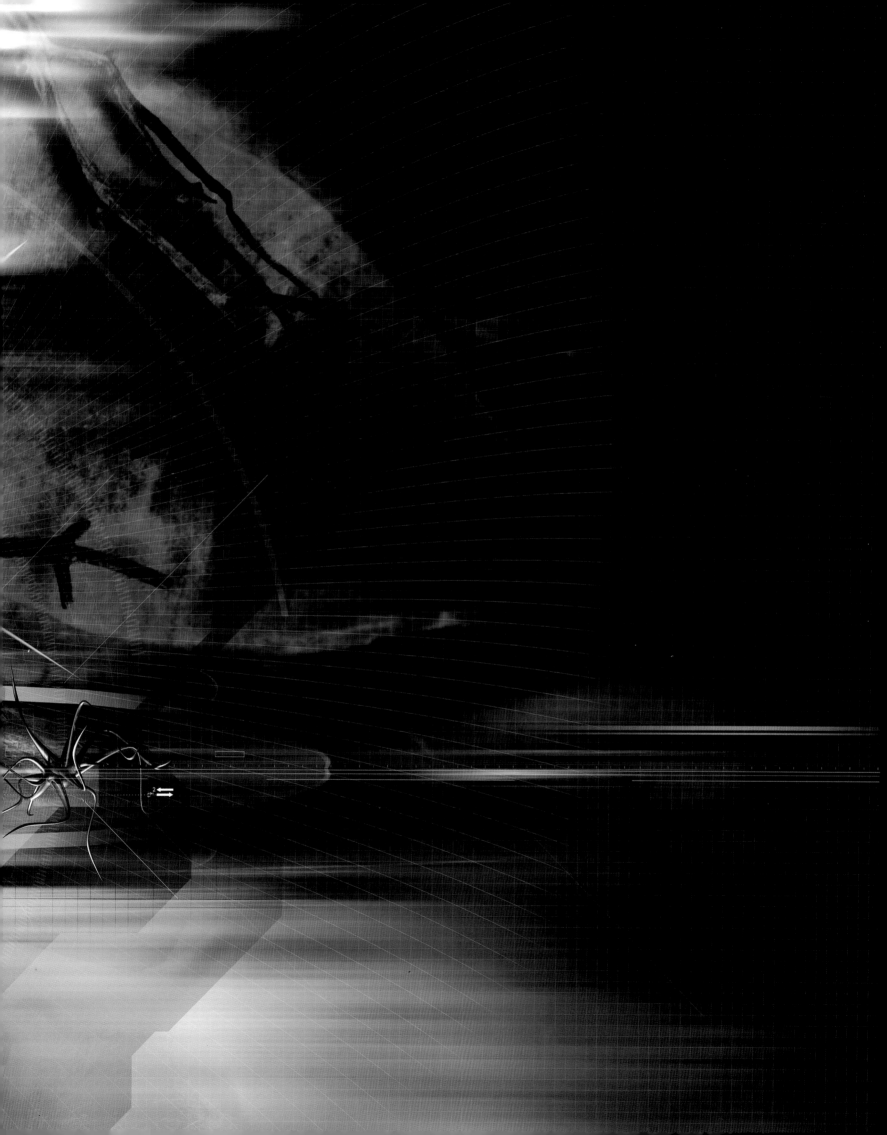

RE-DEFINING THE ICEAGE

RE-DEFINES THE FUTURE

artist/company:	**Andreas Lindholm,** Brainreactor
artwork title:	Iceage

software used:	Photoshop, FreeHand, Cinema 4D
comments:	Cold as Mars

artist/company: **Andreas Lindholm,** Brainreactor

artwork title: Silence

software used: Photoshop, FreeHand, Cinema 4D

comments: Hot as hell

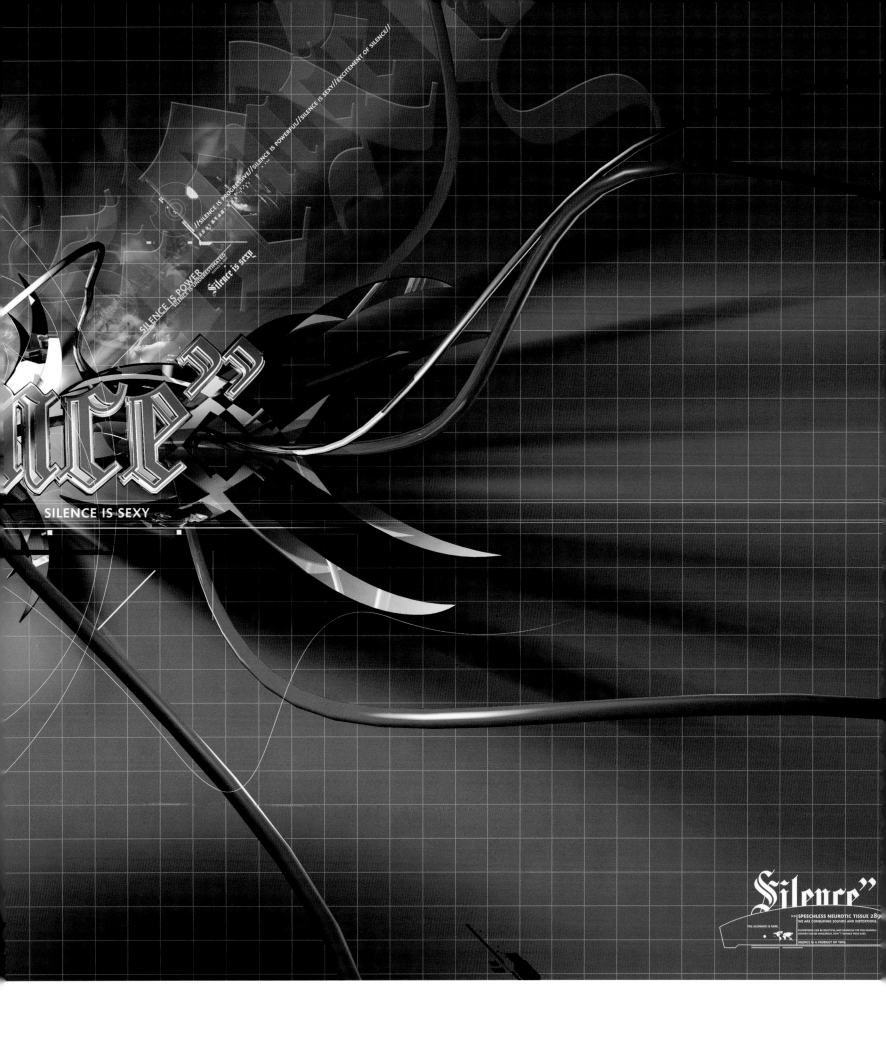

SILENCE IS SEXY

Silence"

artist/company: **Andreas Lindholm,** Brainreactor

artwork title: Metalspread 01

software used: Photoshop, FreeHand, Strata StudioPro

comments: The birth of MetalHeart

622 millimeters

567 millimeters

BOOSTER

/there´s/no/creative/limits/use/your/imagination/index.html

m e t a l h e a r t

[a Distruneactor emBOX project]

artist/company: **Andreas Lindholm,** Brainreactor

artwork title: Metalspread 02

software used: Photoshop, FreeHand, Strata StudioPro

comments: To messy to explain

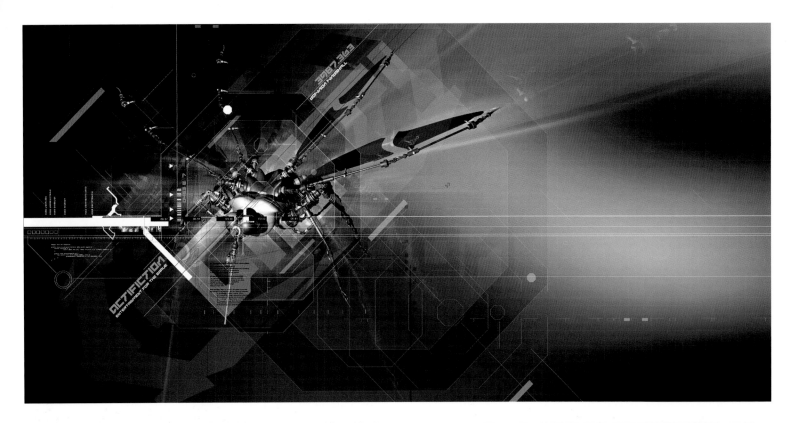

artist/company: **Andreas Lindholm,** Brainreactor

artwork title: Various illustrations and experiments

software used: Photoshop, FreeHand, various 3D applications

comments: Commercial work

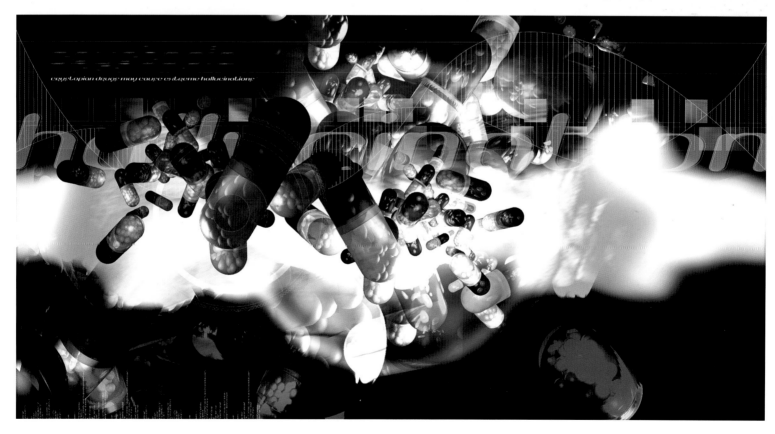

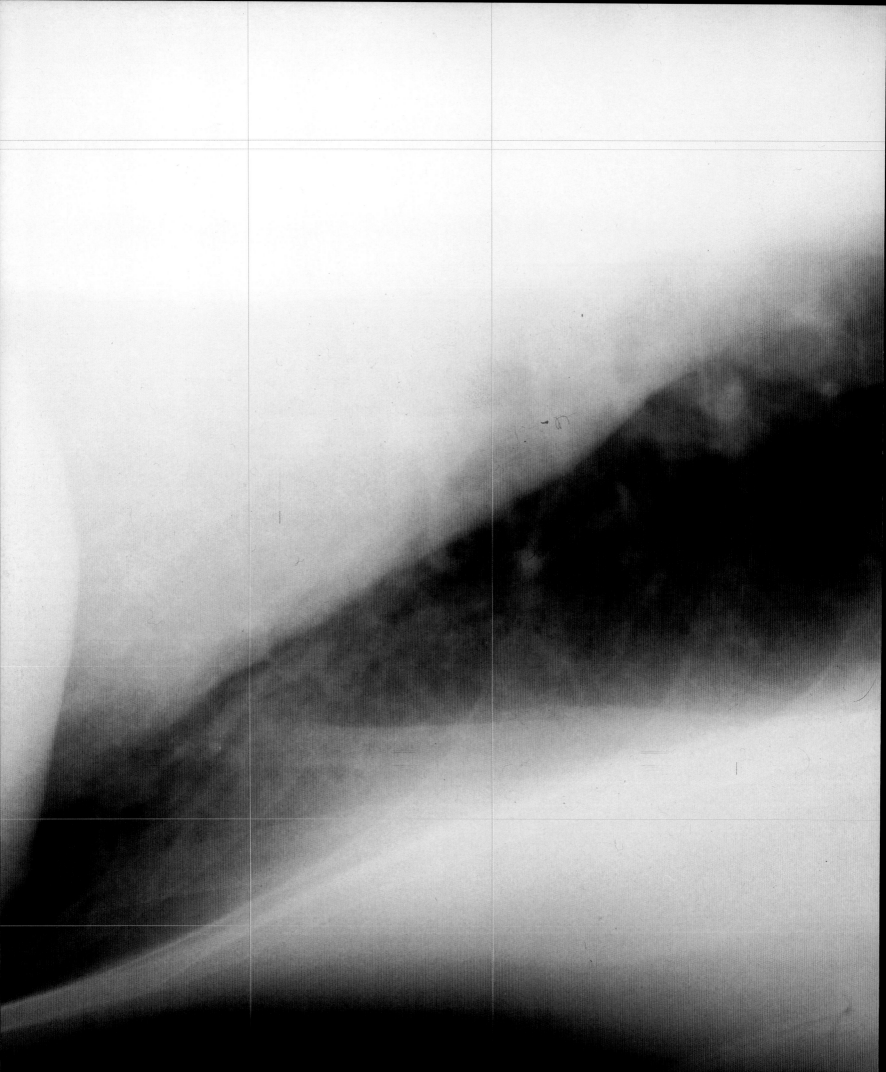

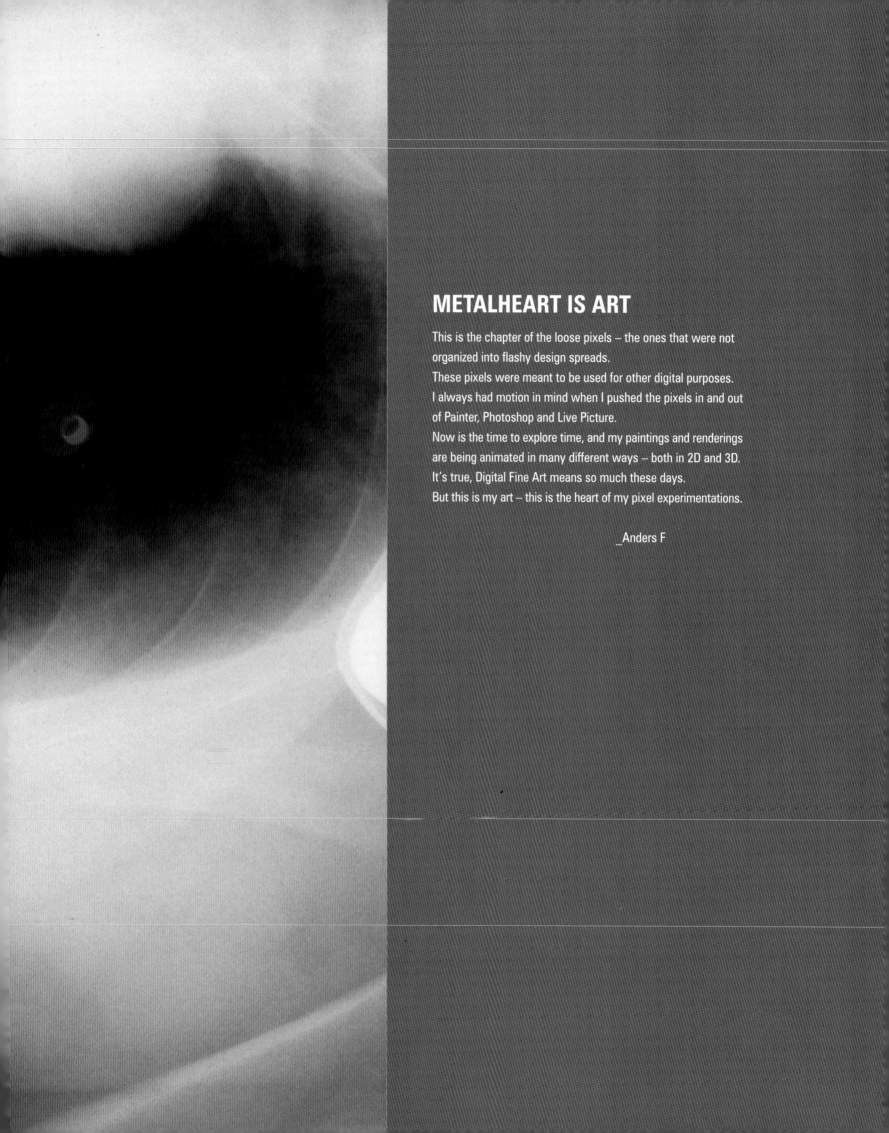

METALHEART IS ART

This is the chapter of the loose pixels – the ones that were not
organized into flashy design spreads.
These pixels were meant to be used for other digital purposes.
I always had motion in mind when I pushed the pixels in and out
of Painter, Photoshop and Live Picture.
Now is the time to explore time, and my paintings and renderings
are being animated in many different ways – both in 2D and 3D.
It's true, Digital Fine Art means so much these days.
But this is my art – this is the heart of my pixel experimentations.

_Anders F

artist/company: **Anders F Rönnblom,** Studio Matchbox   software used: Photoshop, Painter, Live Picture

artwork titles: Monk and the Cyberbabies, Ghost Glass No 5

artist/company:	**Anders F Rönnblom,** Studio Matchbox	software used:	Photoshop, TextureScape, Terrazzo, Painter, Live Picture
artwork titles:	Getting To The Extra Church On Time 1 & 2	comments:	Work in proress: images from an animated art video sequence

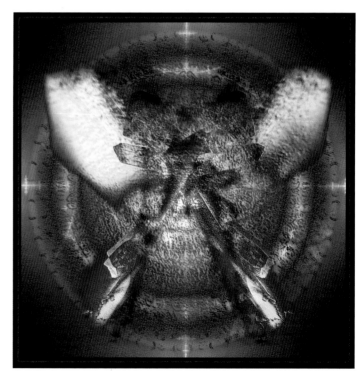

artist/company: **Anders F Rönnblom,** Studio Matchbox   software used: Photoshop, TextureScape, Terrazzo, Painter, Live Picture

artwork titles: The Equizinelle Series, Monk's missing, Blond Equize

comments: Work in proress: images from an animated art video sequence

Photo by Mariann Eklund

artist/company: **Anders F Rönnblom,** Studio Matchbox   software used: Painter, Live Picture, Pixar Typestry, Photoshop

artwork titles: Spotlight Eggs 1 & 2, RenderMan Sculpture 8

artist/company: **Anders F Rönnblom,** Studio Matchbox

software used: Pixar Typestry, Live Picture, Photoshop

artwork titles: RenderMan Sculpture 5 & 6

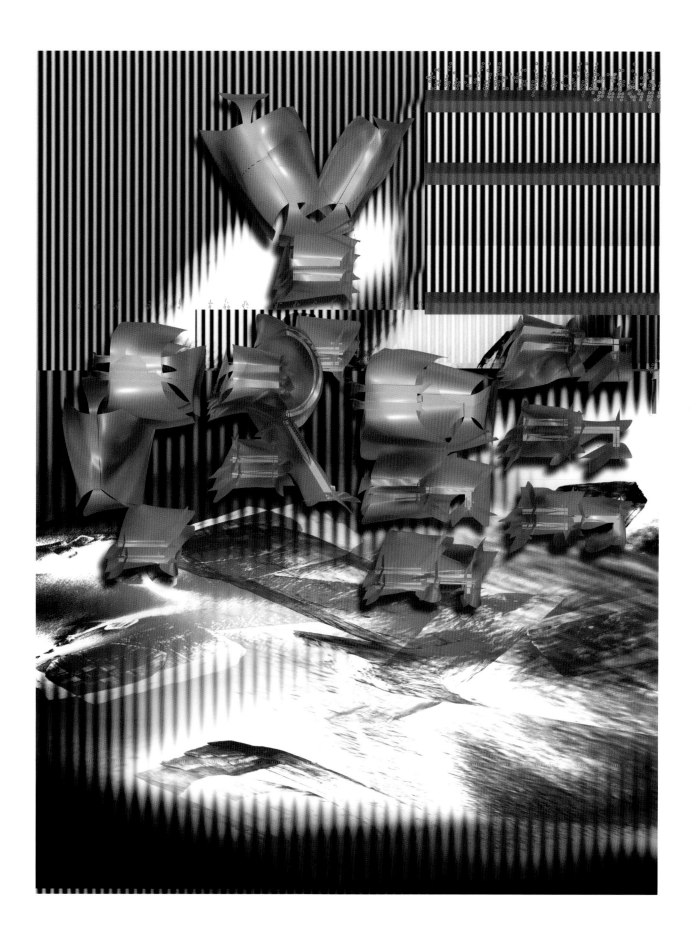

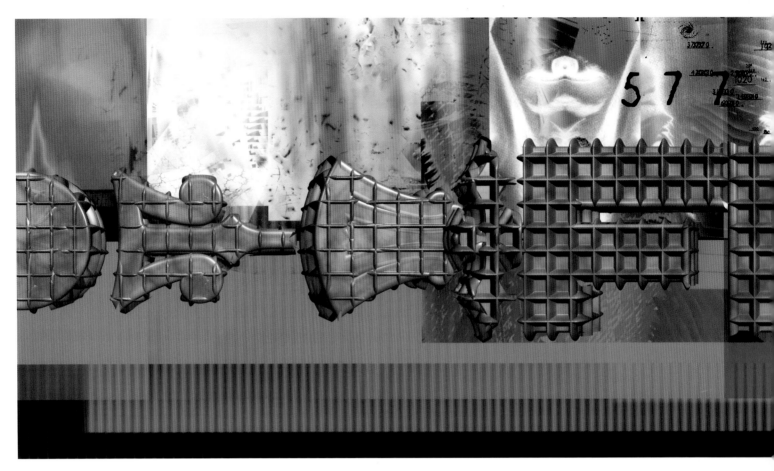

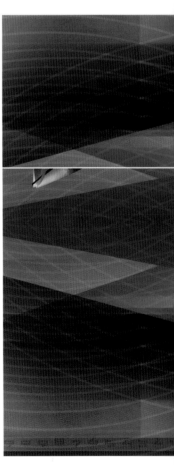

artist/company: **Anders F Rönnblom,** Studio Matchbox   software used: Pixar Typestry, Live Picture, Illustrator, Photoshop

artwork titles: RenderMan Sculpture 7 & 1

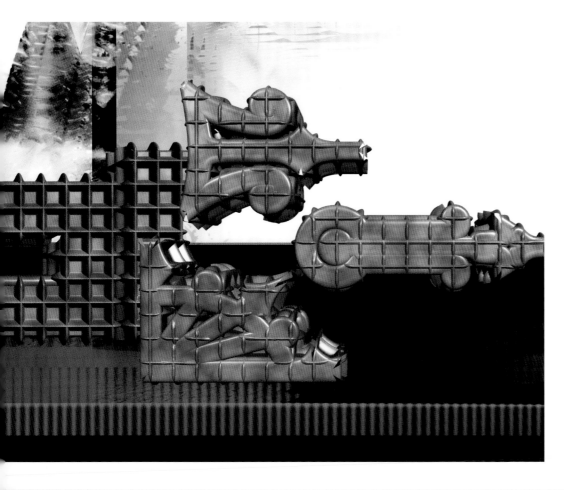

artist/company: **Anders F Rönnblom,** Studio Matchbox

software used: Photoshop, Painter, Live Picture

artwork titles: Statues in Trasition 1, 2 & 3

comments: Work in proress: images from an animated art video sequence

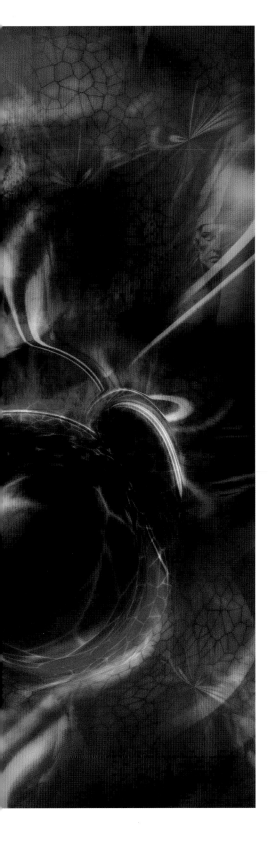
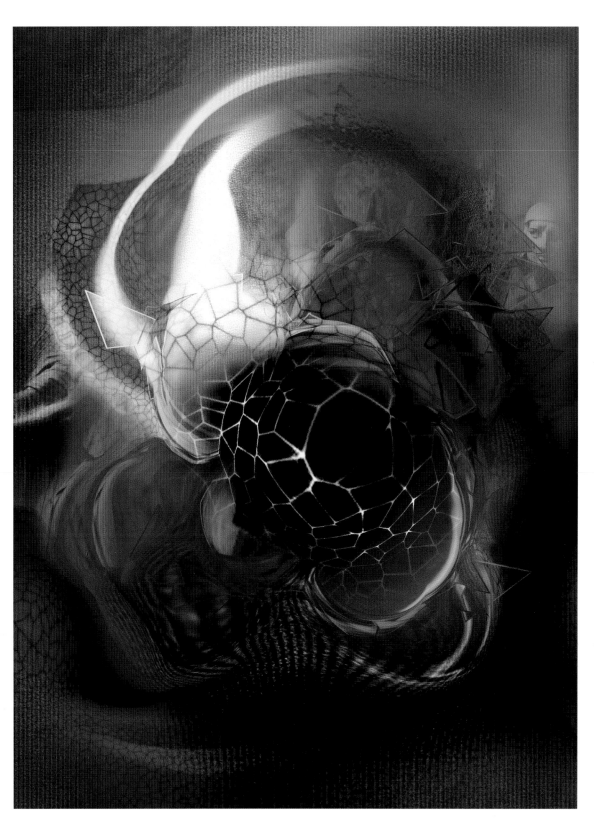

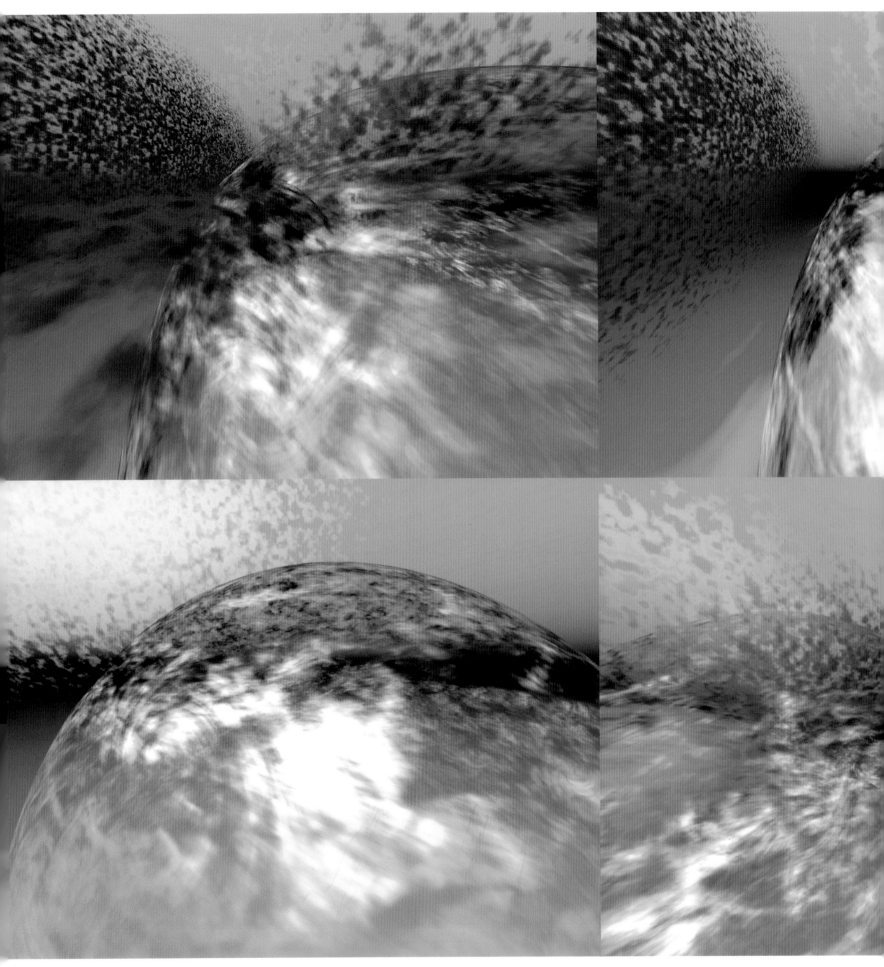

artist/company:	**Anders F Rönnblom,** Studio Matchbox	software used:	Bryce 3D
artwork title:	Clouds Go Nowhere	comments:	Work in proress: images from an animated art video sequence

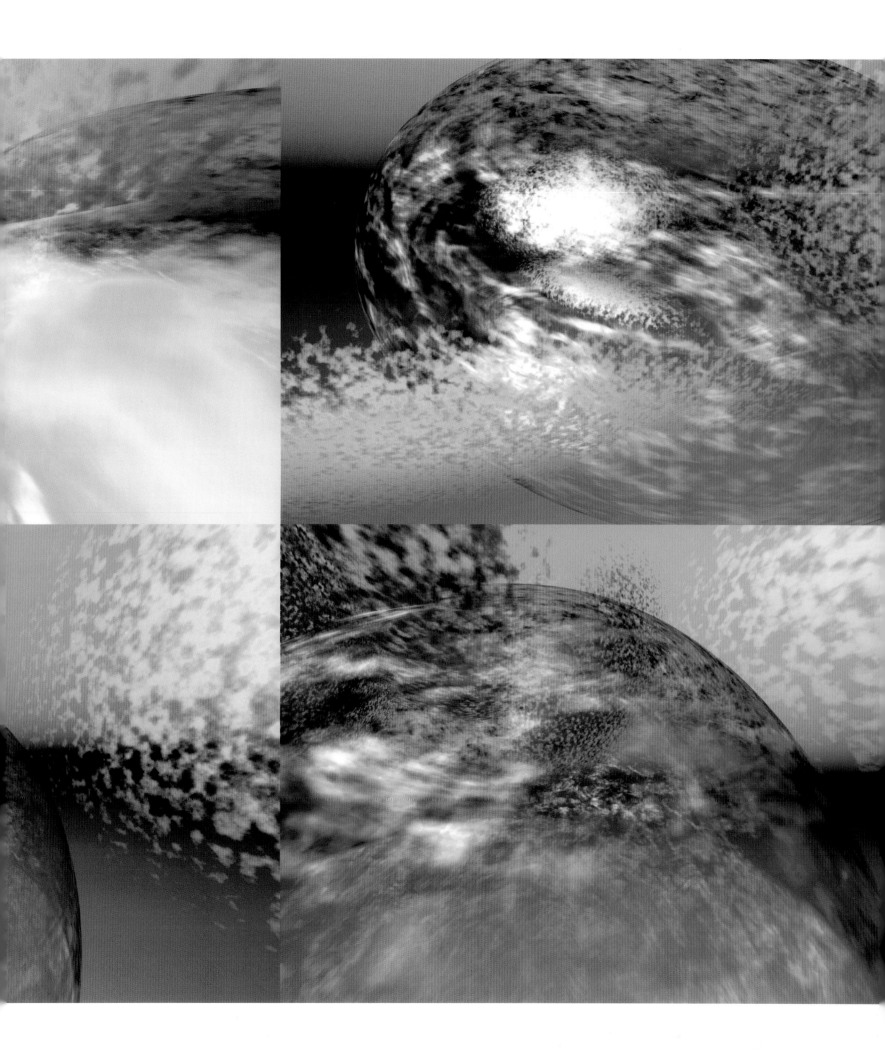

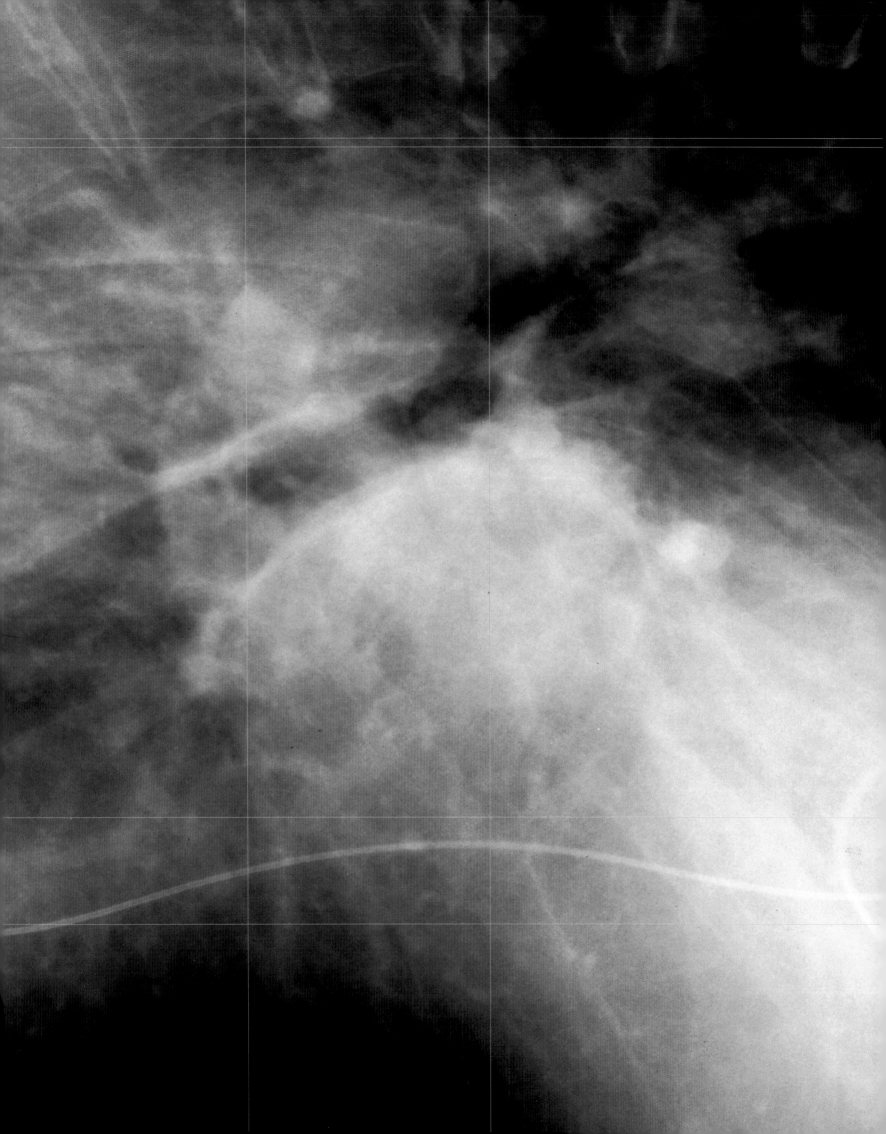

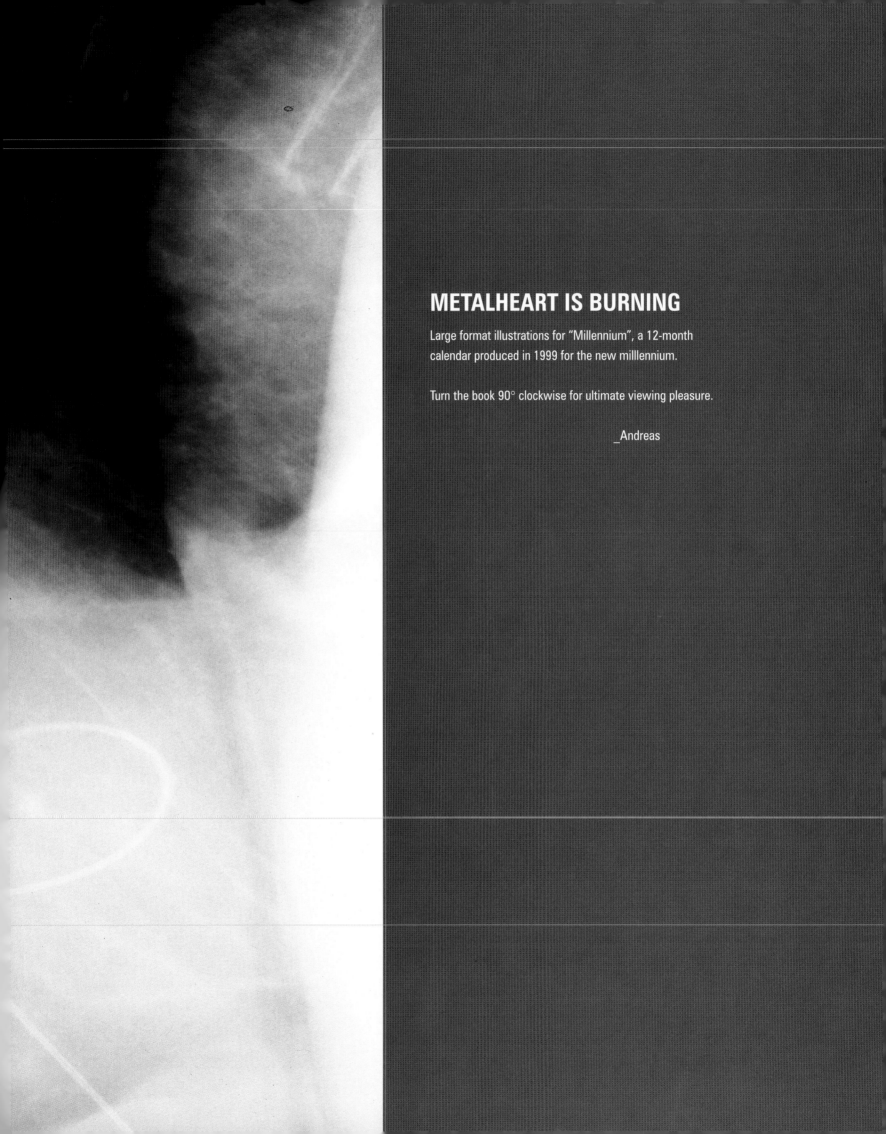

METALHEART IS BURNING

Large format illustrations for "Millennium", a 12-month
calendar produced in 1999 for the new milllennium.

Turn the book 90° clockwise for ultimate viewing pleasure.

_Andreas

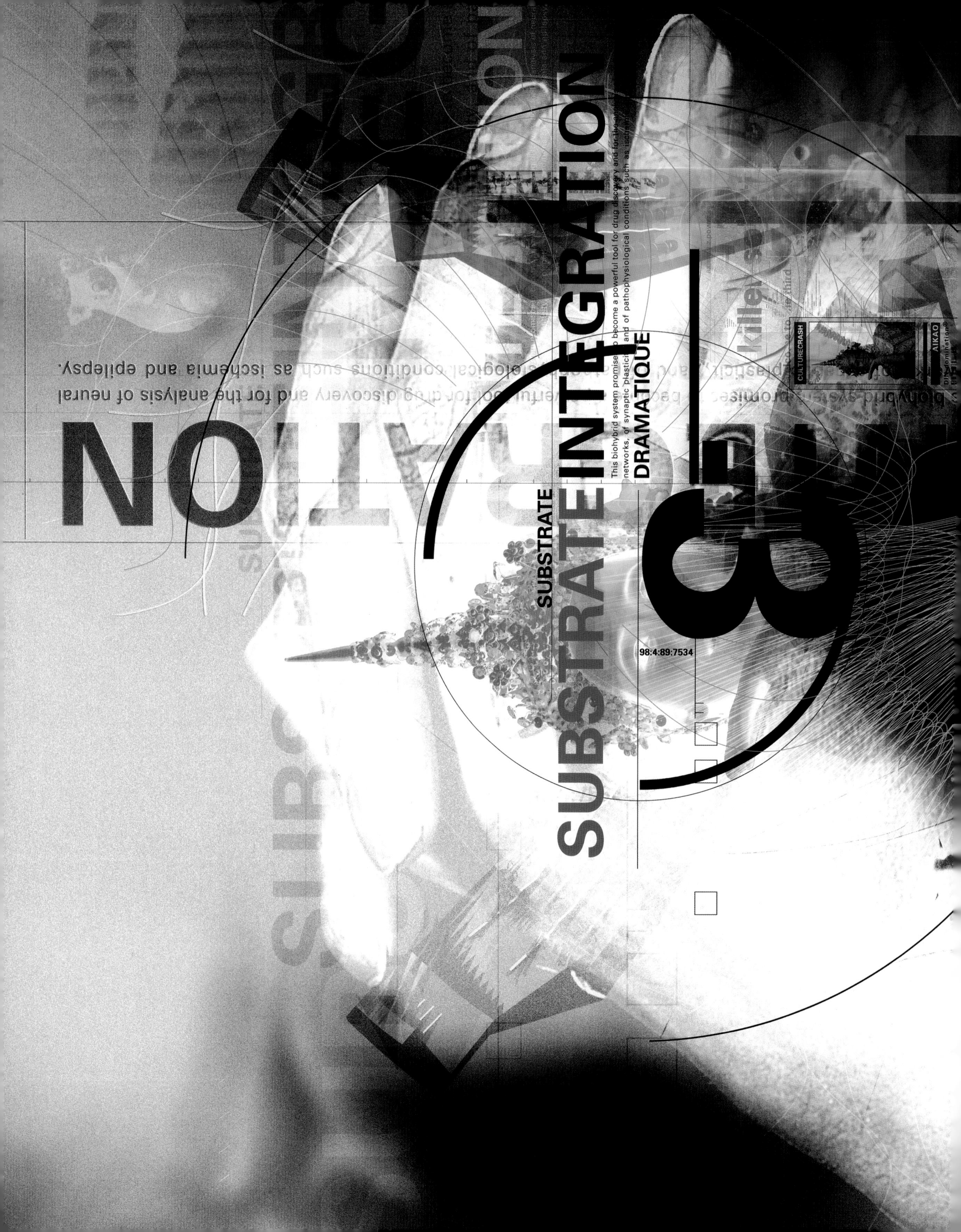

SUBSTRATE
SUBSTRATEINTEGRATION
This biohybrid system promises to become a powerful tool for drug discovery and for the analysis of neural networks, of synaptic plasticity and of pathophysiological conditions such as ischemia and epilepsy.
DRAMATIQUE
98:4:89:7534
3
ATION
for the analysis of neural
such as ischemia and epilepsy.
CULTURECRASH
AIKAO
killer

98:4:89:7534

SUBS

FULLSANS

SUBS

FULLSANS

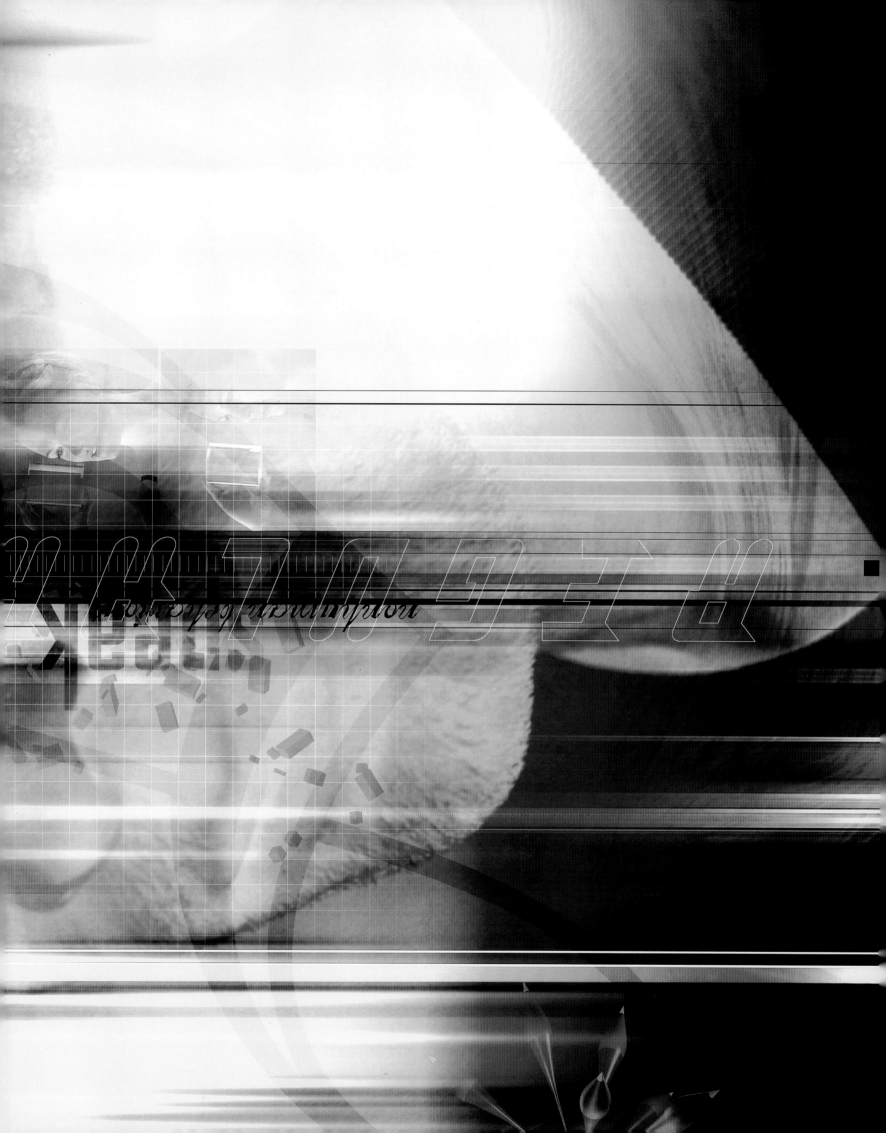

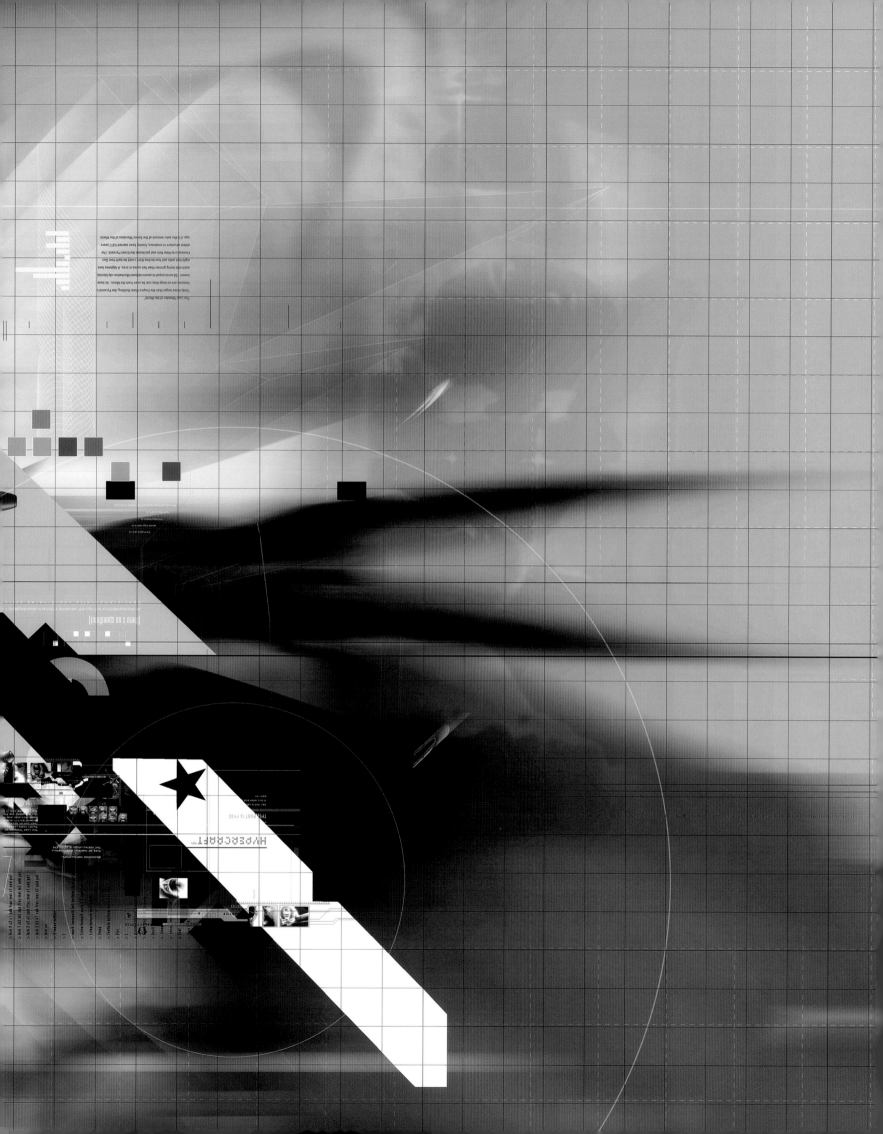

HVPE3CA3FT™

distortions

//permedia/analythic/solutions/for/the/brave

43984:44

>>18.99.992

>>17.63.381

>>16.78.290

>>14.37.304

UNKNOWN LANGUA
3
E INCREDIBLE ACCURACY OF THE PYRAMID S CONSTRUCTION WAS THE GREAT SCIENTIST AND MATHEMATICIAN SIR ISAAC NEWTON. ATTEMPING TO FORMULATE HIS FAMOUS LAW OF GRAVITY, NEWTON NEEDED TO KNOW THE DIAMETER OF THE EARTH. H
SINCE NEWTON THEORIZED THAT THE EARTH S SPIN WOULD CAUSE AN EQUATORIAL BULGE. HAVING HEARD LEGENDS CLAIMING THAT KNOWLEDGE OF THE EARTH, THE PAST, AND THE FUTURE WERE CONTAINED IN THE PYRAMID, NEWTON SET OUT TO

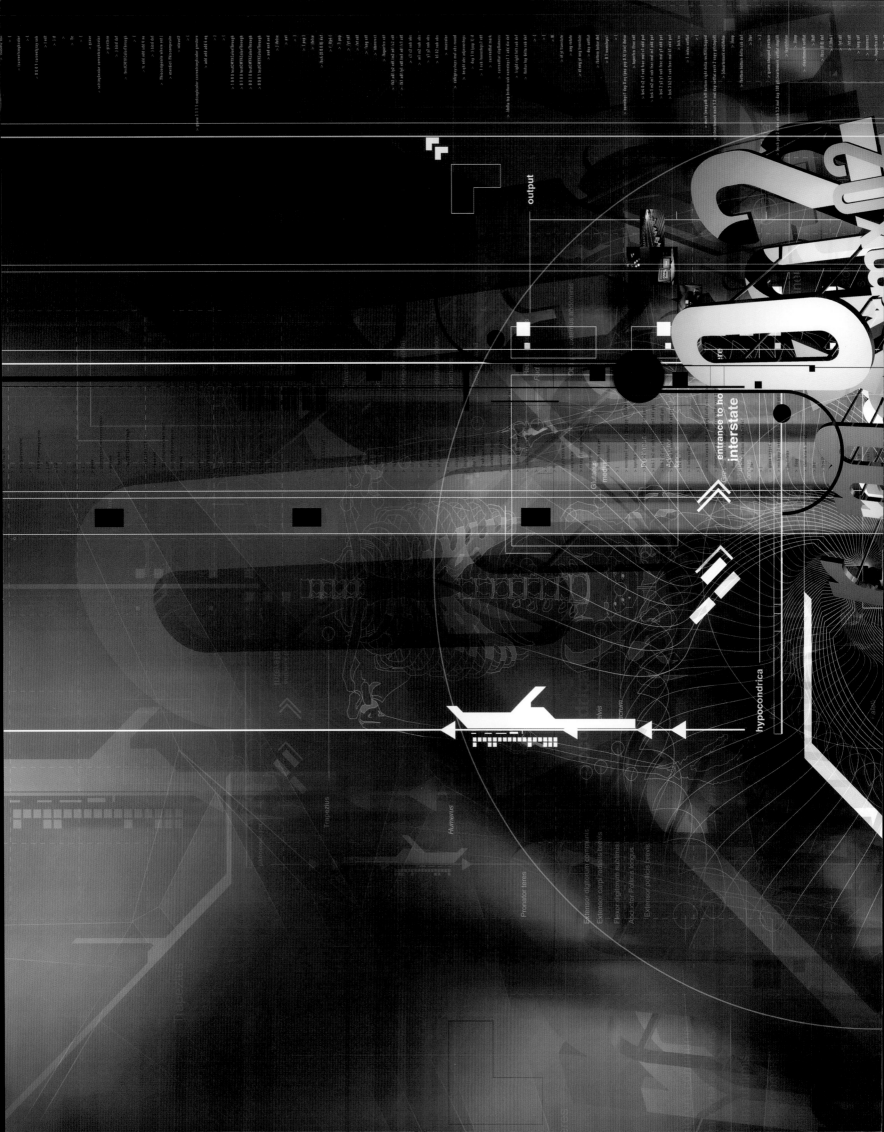

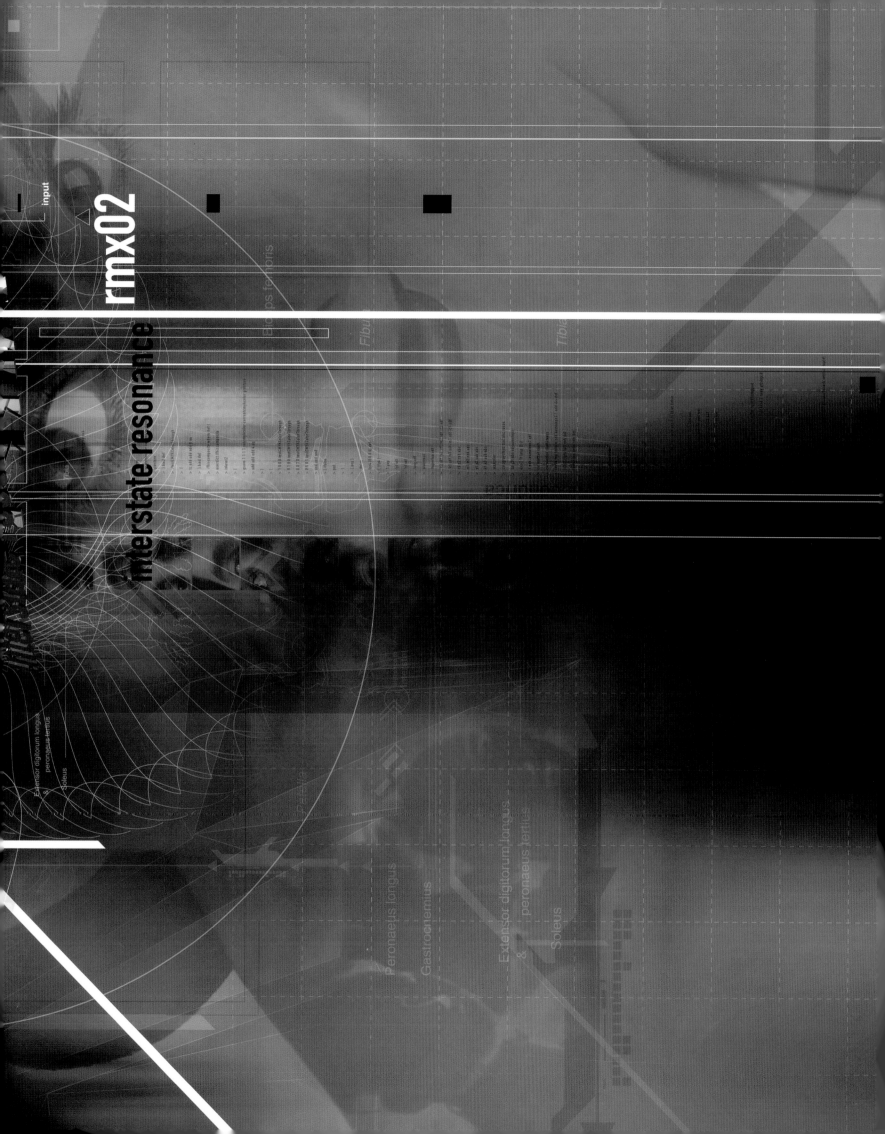

input

rmx02

interstate resonance

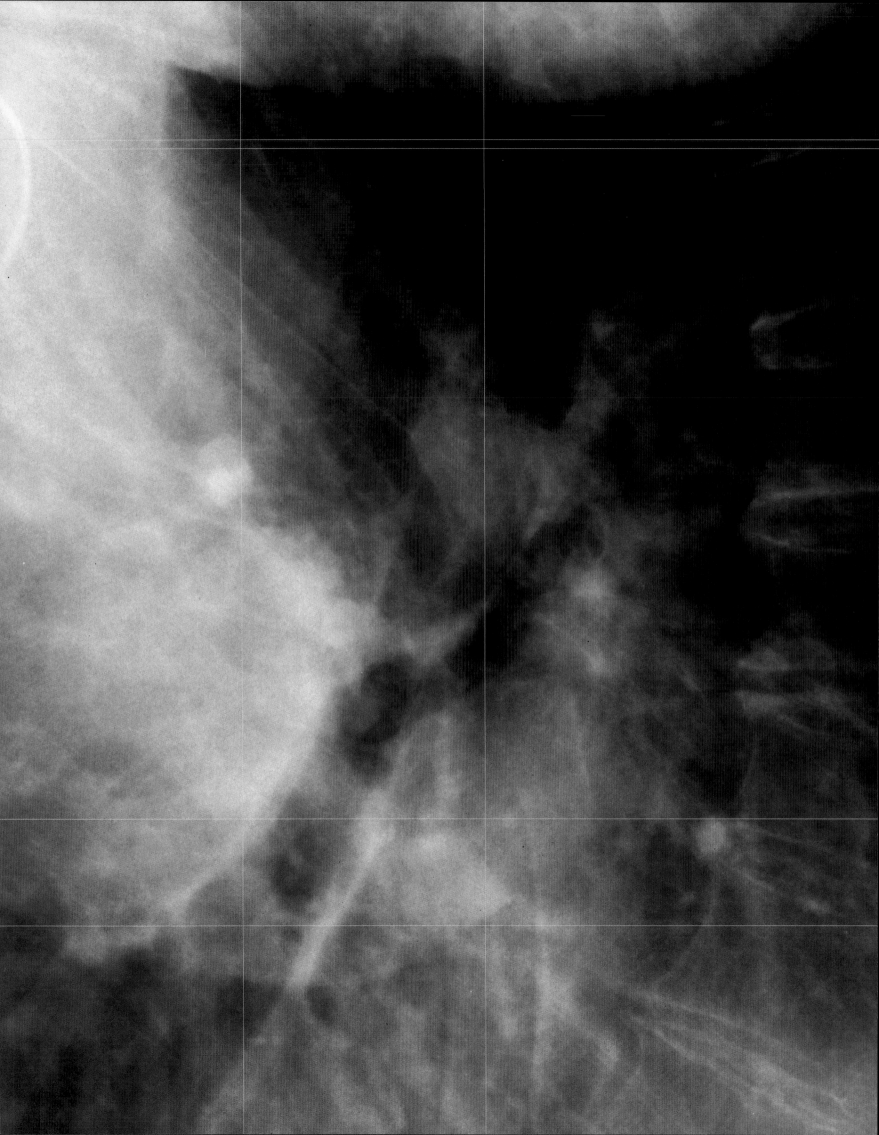

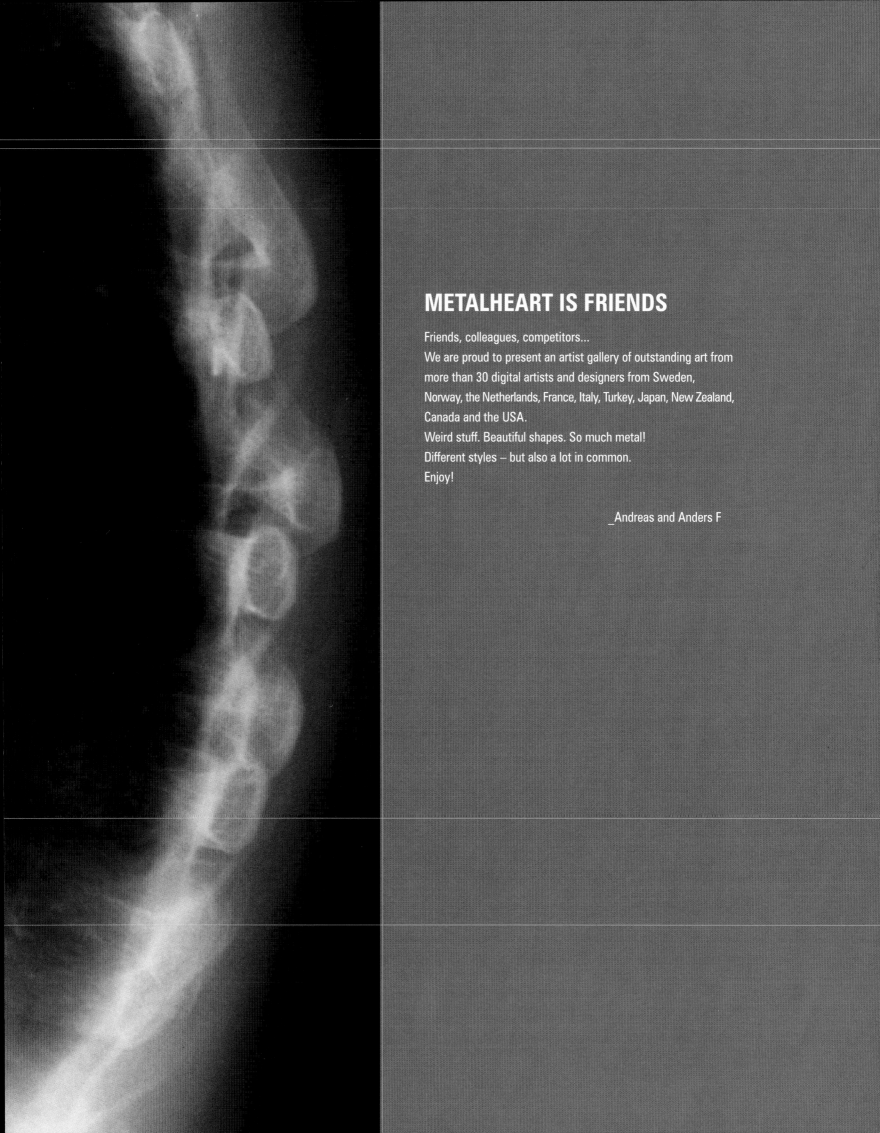

METALHEART IS FRIENDS

Friends, colleagues, competitors...
We are proud to present an artist gallery of outstanding art from
more than 30 digital artists and designers from Sweden,
Norway, the Netherlands, France, Italy, Turkey, Japan, New Zealand,
Canada and the USA.
Weird stuff. Beautiful shapes. So much metal!
Different styles – but also a lot in common.
Enjoy!

_Andreas and Anders F

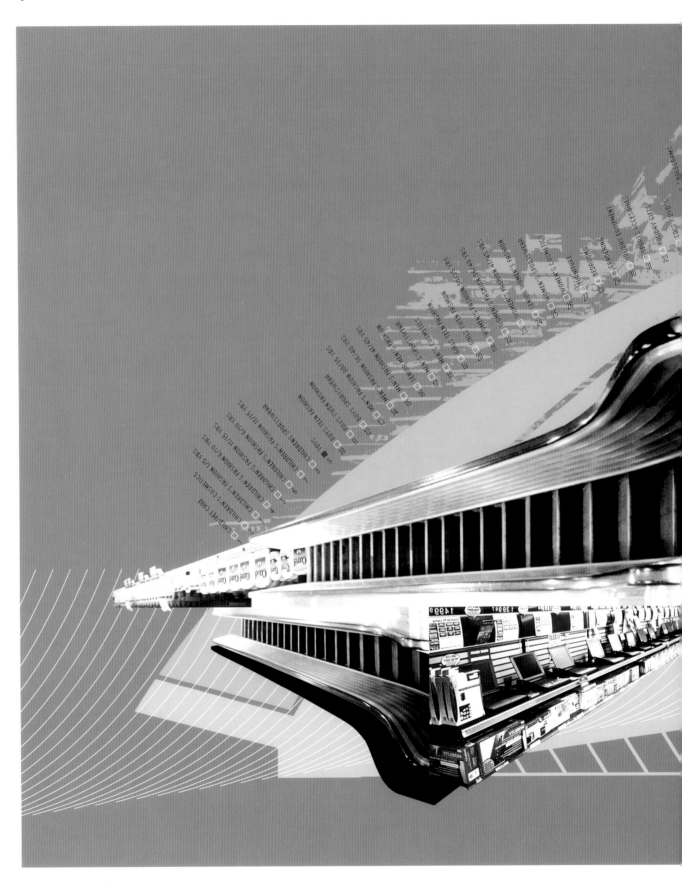

artists/company:	**Bas Waijers and Jurgen van Zachten,** Riff Raff
based in:	Amsterdam, the Netherlands
artwork title:	Shopping
software used:	Illustrator, Photoshop, QuarkXPress, Infini-D
contact info:	www.riffraff.nl

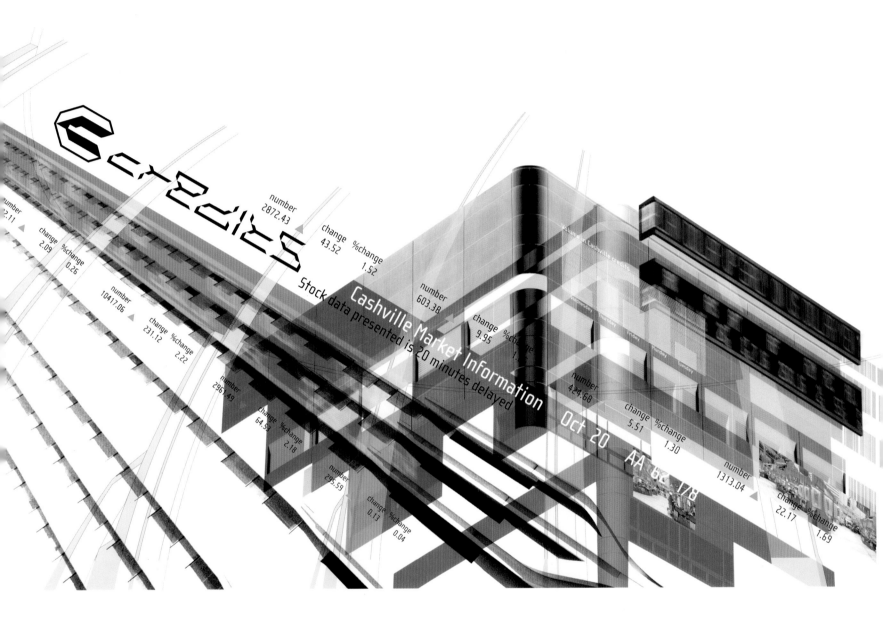

artists/company:	**Bas Waijers and Jurgen van Zachten,** Riff Raff
based in:	Amsterdam, The Netherlands
artwork titles:	Financial, Mailing, Planologie
software used:	Illustrator, Photoshop, QuarkXPress, Infini-D
contact info:	www.riffraff.nl

artists/company: **Bas Waijers and Jurgen van Zachten,** Riff Raff

based in: Amsterdam, the Netherlands

artwork titles: Architecture 3, Architecture 1

software used: Illustrator, Photoshop, QuarkXPress, Infini-D

contact info: www.riffraff.nl

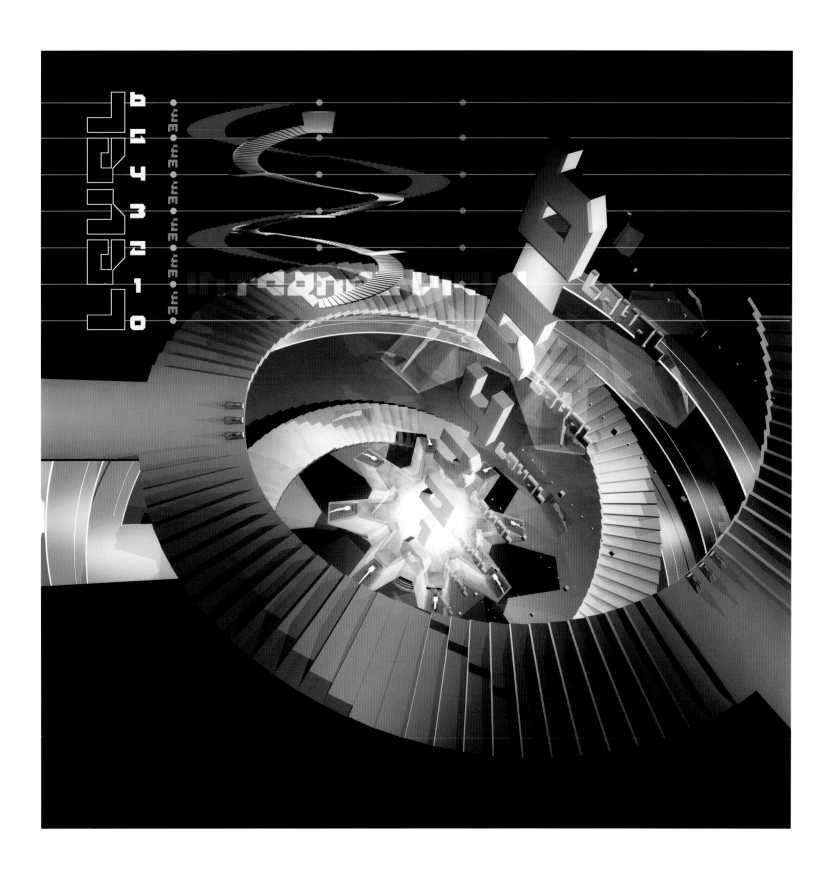

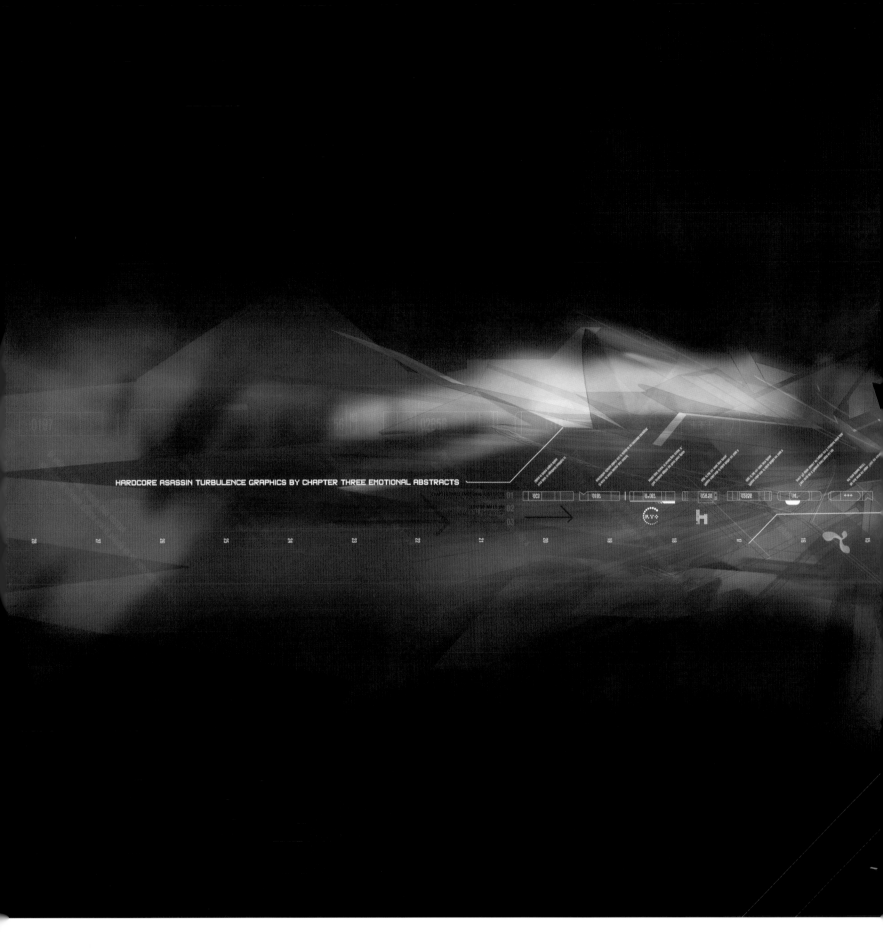

HARDCORE ASASSIN TURBULENCE GRAPHICS BY CHAPTER THREE EMOTIONAL ABSTRACTS

artist/company: **Jens Karlsson**

based in: Karlskrona, Sweden

artwork title: Industrial Intelligence

software used: Photoshop

contact info: jens@chapter3.net

[deathcold]

BEYOND THE PHYSICAL BODY EXISTS ANOTHER MANIFESTATION OF US (ANOTHER MANIFESTATION OF ME)

INDUSTRIAL INTELLIGENCE 48:3

IDIORYTHMIC EXPRESSION FOR SELF PROMOTION
PLEASE VISIT CHAPTER3.NET RIGHT AWAY

*THINK-063

SPIRITUAL KNOWLEDGE

IT'S JUST REALIZATION THAT YOU'RE GET BEYOND THE TIME OF ETERNITY
SO OPEN IF YOU'RE KIND AND GROWN INSIDE YOUR INDIVIDUAL BELIEF AND
YOU WILL SEE THAT A PERSON WHOSE NEVER GOES OUTSIDE HIS OWN
VILLAGE ALWAYS THINKS HIS VILLAGE IS THE WHOLE WORLD

RIGHTOUSSNESS IN A CROOKED FUTURE
COPYLEFT 2000 **JENS KARLSSON** | CH3

DEMOLOVE PRESENTS

20
00

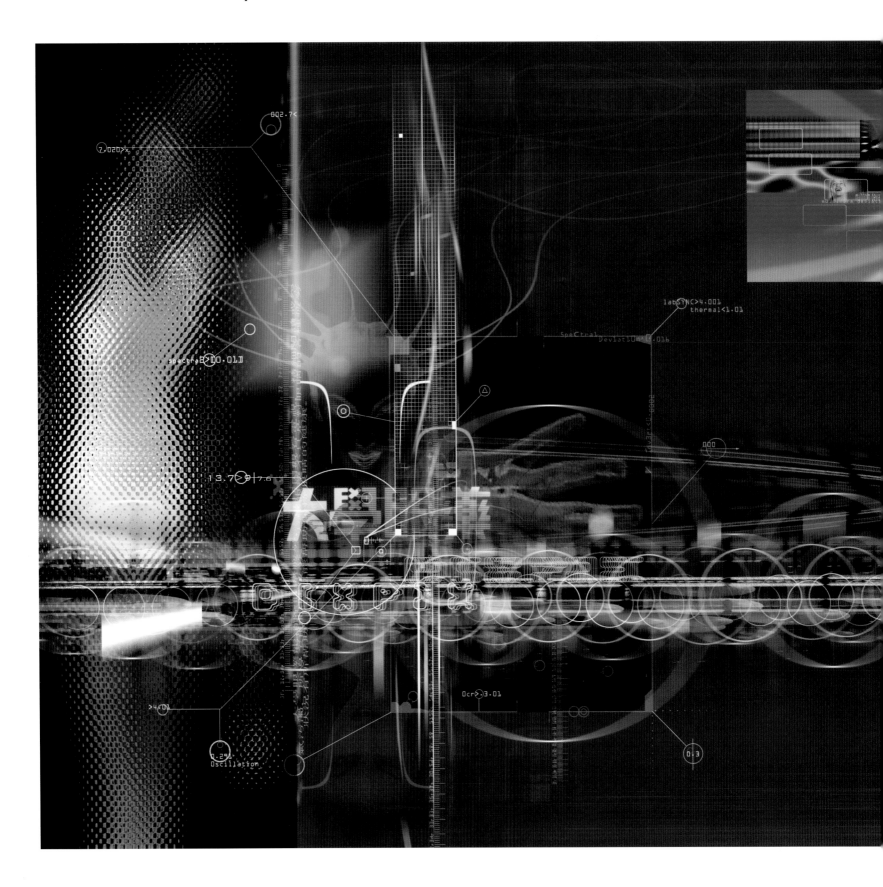

artist/company:	**Richard Krall**
based in:	New York, USA
artwork titles:	Spectral Deviation, Dixpix card, Rocketlogix
software used:	Photoshop
contact info:	dixpix@earthlink.net

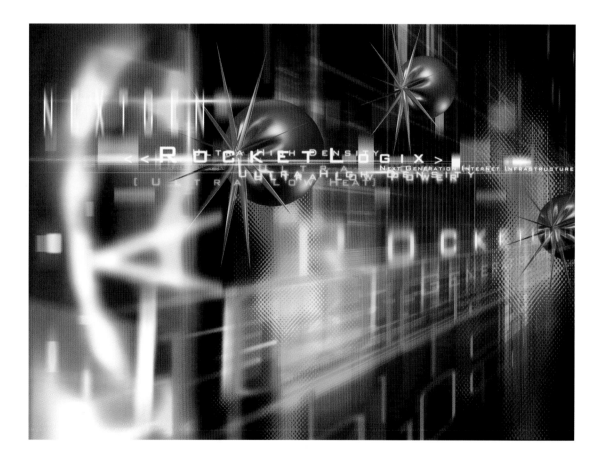

artist/company:	**Klas Jonsson,** Strobe
based in:	Stockholm, Sweden
artwork title:	Ultraviolence
software used:	Photoshop, Cinema 4D
contact info:	klas@strobe.se

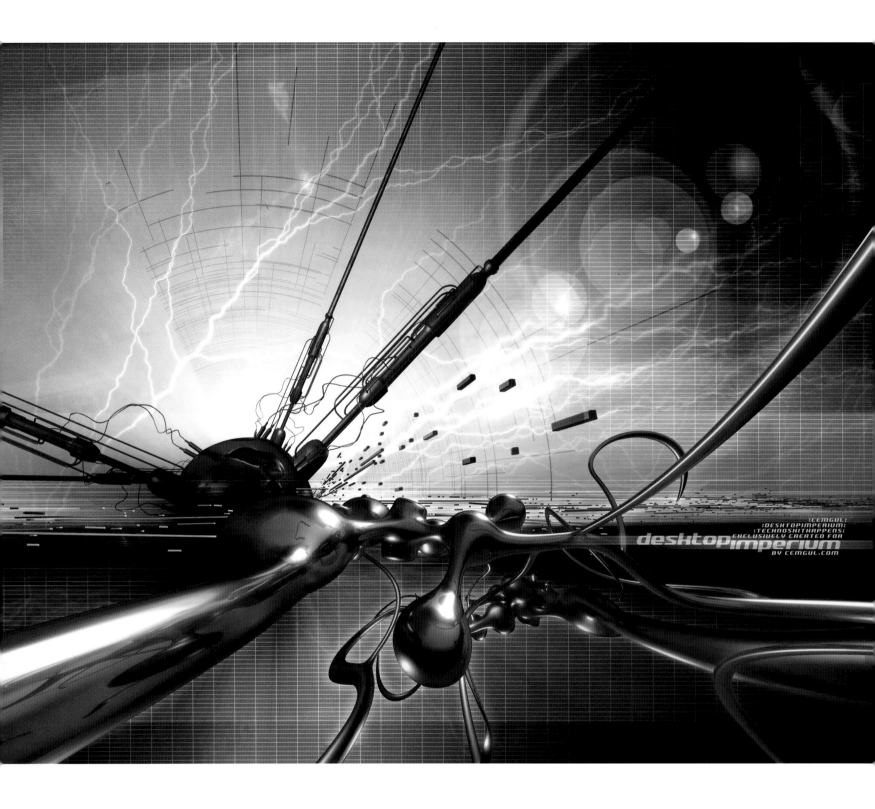

artist/company:	**Cem Gül**, Metropolis
based in:	Ankara, Turkey
artwork titles:	Technoshit Happens, Total Felch
software used:	FreeHand, Photoshop, LightWave 3D
contact info:	mail@cemgul.com

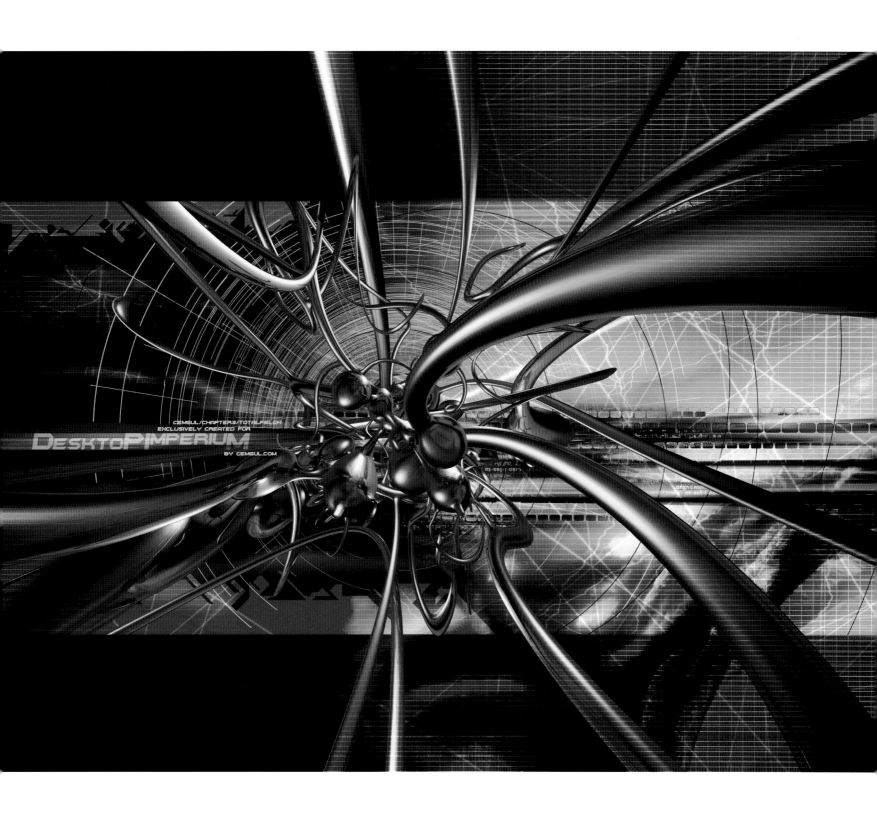

CEMGUL/CHAPTER3/TOTALFIELD
EXCLUSIVELY CREATED FOR
DESKTOPIMPERIUM
BY CEMGUL.COM

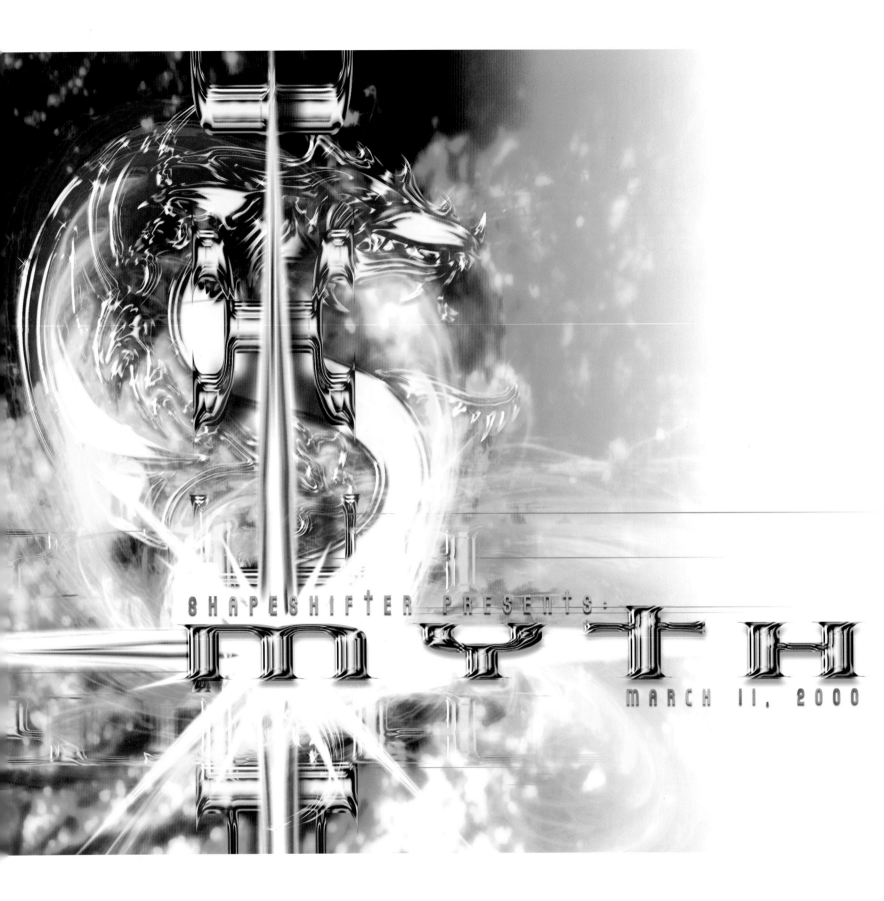

SHAPESHIFTER PRESENTS: MYTH

MARCH 11, 2000

artist/company:	**Cameron Redwine**
based in:	Atlanta, GA, USA
artwork titles:	Myth flyer, Paul van Dyk flyer
contact info:	cameron@one3.com

PLEAZURE IS PLEASED TO PRESENT HIS ONLY ATLANTA APPEARANCE
AN EVENING WITH PAUL VAN DYK ON THURSDAY DECEMBER NINTH
SPINNING AN EXTENDED THREE HOUR SET

PLEAZURE PRESENTS
THURSDAY DECEMBER NINTH, NINETEEN NINETY NINE

PAUL VAN DYK
MUTE /GERMANY

DJ SYNC
SATELLITE / DARK FORCE NETWORK

GENE CARBONELL
BALANCE / LUNAR

18 + WELCOME | DOOR PRICE: $13 WITH A 1998 PLEAZURE CARD
$14 W/ A 1999 PLEAZURE CARD | $15 W/OUT A PLEAZURE CARD
FOR A FREE PLEAZURE CARD, SIGN UP ON OUR WEB SITE OR
INFO LINE: WWW.PLEAZURE.NET & 770.492.0912
THE WAREHOUSE | 339 MARIETTA ST, ATLANTA, GA

DIRECTIONS FROM I-75 / 85: TAKE EXIT 100 (NORTH AVE) AND TURN RIGHT
(TRAVELING WEST FROM MIDTOWN). AT 2ND LIGHT, TURN LEFT ON LUCKIE ST.
THE WAREHOUSE IS APPROX 1 MILE DOWN ON THE RIGHT (1 BLOCK BEFORE YOU
GET TO NIKE EXPO).   DESIGN: CAMERON REDWINE

software used: Illustrator, Photoshop, KPT3/5/6, Bryce

comments: "A majority of what I do is related to music and nightlife – the promotion for raves, clubs, bars and pubs."

artist/company:	**Sin Takahashi,** Branz Hatch
based in:	Tokyo, Japan
artwork title:	Digital Solution 98
software used:	Illustrator, Photoshop, 3D Studio Max, Premiere
contact info:	bullcall@mango.ifnet.or.jp

artist/company:	**Toru Kosaka,** Studio EggMan
based in:	Tokyo, Japan
artwork title:	Joints
software used:	Illustrator, Photoshop, Shade III
contact info:	eggman@air.linkclub.or.jp

debris

the right brain is colonized by the left brain which is colonized by language which is colonized by society which maintains the status quo

HAL

OTAN

Widows 2000 Professional

design/illustration: halvor bodin aka superlow (http://www.superlow.com). fonts: amp by superlow, proxima parada by berdt ottem, + akodenz grotesk. photography by johan wichagen, observatoriet, sebastian ludvigsen, marcel leliemhof ++

ich weiss natuerlich: einzig durch glueck habe ich so viele freunde ueberlebt. aber heute nacht im traum hörte ich diese freunde von mir sagen: »die staerkeren ueberleben« und ich hasste mich...

an alliance concerned mainly with collective defence to one which will be a guarantee of security in europe and an upholder of democratic values both within and beyond our borders.

the joystick of the western democracies has become encrusted with the blood of its wonderful freedom from responsibilities. everyone, everyone plays and someone else pays...

ewige wilderkehr des gleichen...

artist/company:	**Halvor Bodin,** Union Design
based in:	Oslo, Norway
artwork title:	Angelus Novus poster
software used:	FreeHand, Photoshop
contact info:	superlow@superlow.no

angelus novus

war
as spectator sport

a klee painting named «angelus novus»
shows an angel looking as though he is
about to move away from something
he is fixedly contemplating.
his eyes are staring, his mouth is open,
his wings are spread.
this is how one pictures the angel of history.

his face is turned toward the past.

where we perceive a chain of events,
he sees one single catastrophe
which keeps piling wreckage upon wreckage
and hurls it in front of his feet.

the angel would like to stay, awaken the dead,
and make whole what has been smashed.
but a storm is blowing from paradise;
it has got caught in his wings with such violence
that the angel can no longer close them.

this storm irresistibly propels him into the future
to which his back is turned,
while the pile of debris before him grows skyward.

this storm is what we call progress.

- walter benjamin

artist/company:	**Halvor Bodin,** Union Design
based in:	Oslo, Norway
artwork title:	Spectator poster
software used:	FreeHand, Photoshop
contact info:	superlow@superlow.no

real art is play.
play is one of the most
immediate of all experiences.
those who have cultivated
the pleasure of play cannot
be expected to give up
simply to make political point.
art will go on, in somewhat
the same sense that
breathing,
eating,
or fucking
will go on...

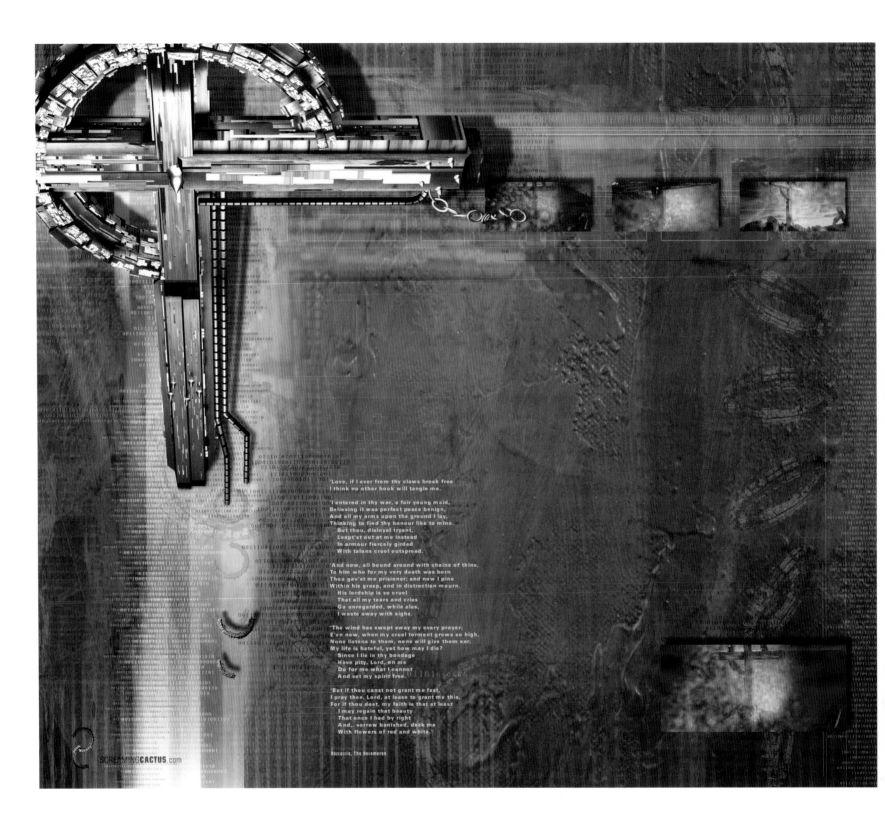

artist/company: **Lou Zadesky,** Screaming Cactus

based in: San Francisco, USA

artwork titles: Rusty C-1, Rusty C-2

software used: Photoshop, 3D Studio Max

contact info: www.ScreamingCactus.com

'With fitting tears, I show
The mourning heart bereaved,
It's faith in Love deceived.

'Love, who first fixed into my heart
She for whom now I sigh in vain;
You showed me her so full of grace
That I held light each bitter pain
  Which came to torment me
  So everlastingly.
  I know my error now;
  Not without grief, I vow.

'I comprehend that false deceit
And see how, while I thought that she
Seemed to allow my love, she'd found
Another servant, spurning me.
  Ah, then I could not see
  My future misery!
  But she the other took
  And me for him forsook

'A mournful song swelled through my heart
When I perceived that I was spurned,
That dwells there still; and oft I curse
Faith, hope, love and the hour I learned
  Her noble beauteousness
  Whose radiance doth oppress
  My dying soul, which yet
  Cannot those charms forget.

'Bereft of every comfort now,
Oh, Lord of love, to you I cry;
I burn with such a torment here
That for a less I'd crave to die.
  Come Death, then, end my life
  With all it's cruel strife;
  Strike down my misery!
  I shall the better be.

'No other way nor other ease
Remains to soothe my grief but death.
Grant me this, Love, and end my woes;
Take from me now my wretched breath.
  All joy is gone from me,
  No pleasure's left for me:
  Make then my death content her,
  As the new love you sent her.

'My song, if none should learn to think to sing
Thee over, I take little care:
No one can sing thee as I can.
Only, to Love one message bear:

  Beg him, since life was all
  Loathsome to me, and vile,
  To safer haven take
  Me for his honour's sake.'

          Boccaccio, The Decameron

SCREAMING**CACTUS**.com

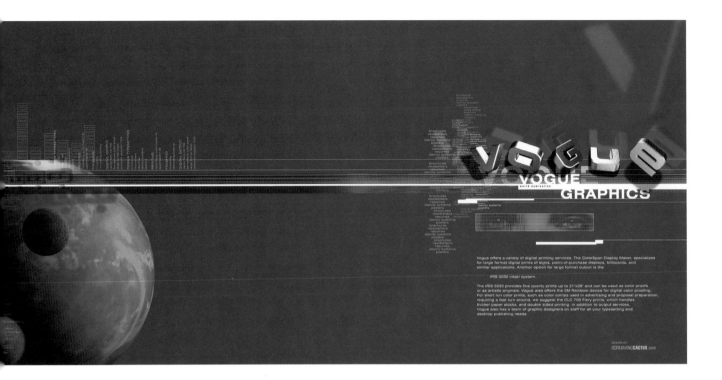

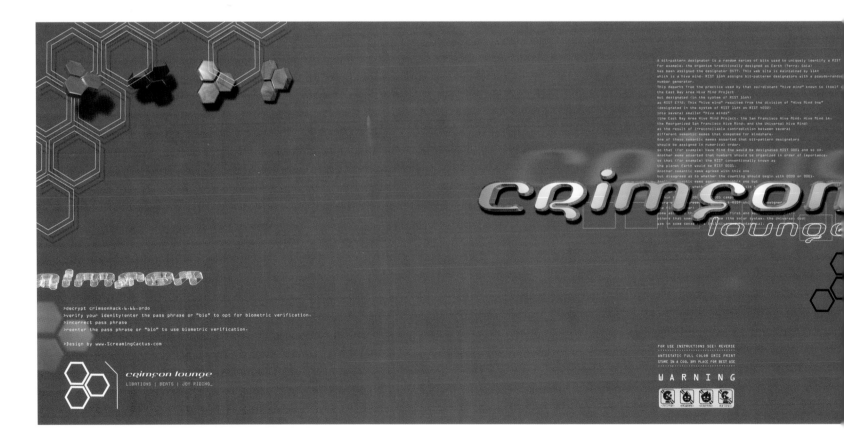

artist/company:	**Lou Zadesky,** Screaming Cactus
based in:	San Francisco, USA
artwork titles:	Vogue Graphics, Crimson Lounge
software used:	Photoshop, 3D Studio Max
contact info:	www.ScreamingCactus.com

artist/company:	**Albert Kiefer,** Sector A Design
based in:	Venlo, the Netherlands
artwork titles:	Amnesty International 40 Years, Sounds
sofware used:	Maya Unlimited, Photoshop, form•Z, ElectricImage
contact info:	sectora@euronet.nl

artist/company:	**Arne Kaupang,** Arne Kaupang Design	software used:	Illustrator, Photoshop, Infini-D
based in:	Oslo, Norway	comments:	Images and design for a CD album and booklet
artwork titles:	Reset "Play", Reset "Makin' Me Feel"		
contact info:	www.akdesign.no		

RESET

MAKIN' ME FEEL

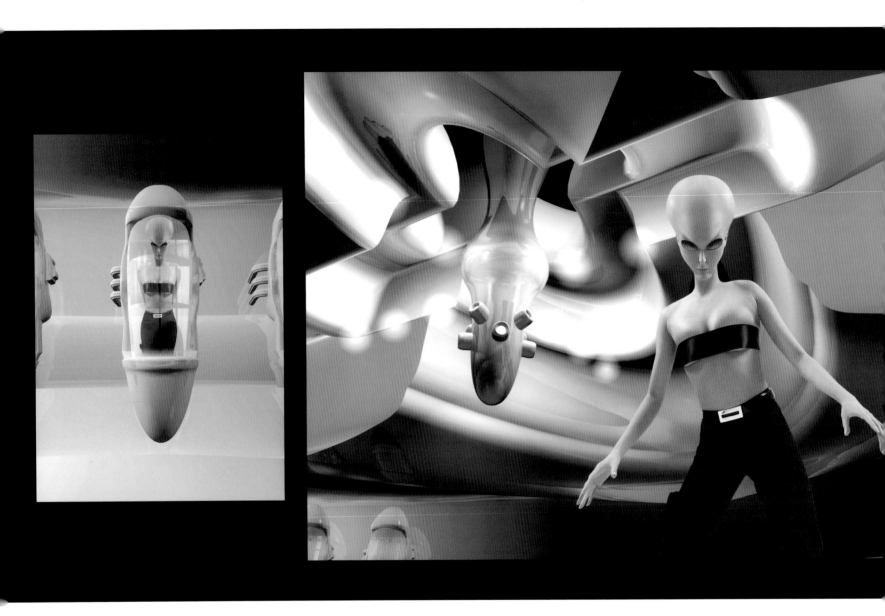

artist/company:	**Arne Kaupang,** Arne Kaupang Design
based in:	Oslo, Norway
artwork title:	Hyperstate
software used:	Illustrator, Photoshop, Infini-D
contact info:	www.akdesign.no

artist/company:	**Torgeir Holm,** Union Design
based in:	Oslo, Norway
artwork titles:	Downloading Soul, Recharging
software used:	Imagine, Photoshop
contact info:	torgeir@union.no

artist/company:	**Tim Jester,** J6Studios
based in:	Houston, TX, USA
artwork title:	Blood (B positive, Don't B Negative)
software used:	Illustrator, KPT Vector Effects, Photoshop, Dimensions
contact info:	jester@j6studios.com

1.

2.

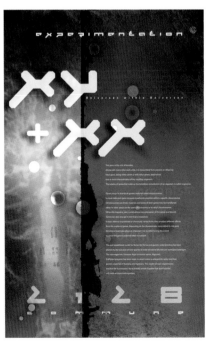

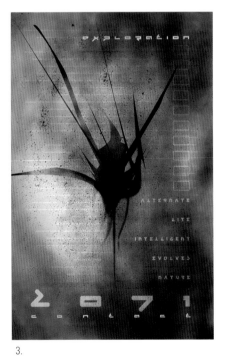

3.

1. artist/company:	**Jim Mousner,** Origin Design	2. artist/company:	**Doni Soward,** D2	3. artist/company:	**Eddy Roberts,** Morphic Resonance
based in:	Houston, TX, USA	based in:	Houston, TX, USA	based in:	Houston, TX, USA
artwork title:	Collage	artwork title:	Poster	artwork titles:	Commune, Contact
software used:	Illustrator, Photoshop	software used:	Illsutrator, Photoshop	software used:	Illustrator, Photoshop
contact info:	mousner@origindesign.com	contact info:	soward@hotmail.com	contact info:	eroberts@minordesign.com

KARAZAN FONT 3D Process Generated
ABCDEFGHIJKabcdefghij0123456

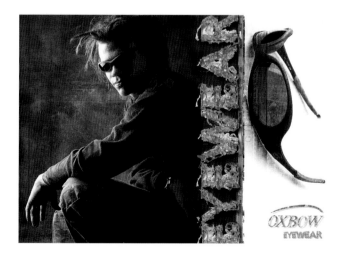

OXBOW
EYEWEAR

artist/company: **Lionel Barat,** Oxbow Promotion

based in: Merignac, France

artwork titles: Bloody Type, Karazan Type, Stream, Eyewear

software used: Pixar Typestry, Photoshop

contact info: lbarat@oxbow.fr

artist/company:	**Leif Åbjörnsson**
based in:	Stockholm, Sweden
artwork titles:	Mr Fix, Mr Clip, Mrs Hook, Mr. T, Mr. Multimedia Robot
software used:	Photoshop, Squizz
contact info:	www.aabjornsson.se

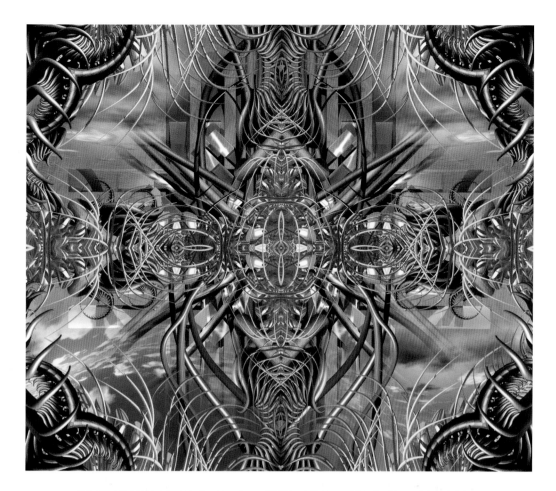

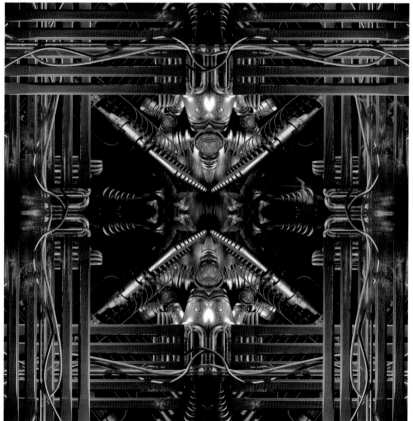

artist/company:	**Robert Zohrab,** Hinge Design
based in:	Auckland, New Zealand
artwork titles:	Organic Window, Intact Instinct
software used:	Photoshop, Strata StudioPro
contact info:	cybcult@ihug.co.nz

artist/company:	**Derek Prospero,** Liquigem
based in:	West Palm Beach, FL, USA
artwork titles:	Vintage, Sepia, Red, Green
software used:	Photoshop
contact info:	www.derekprospero.com

Julius Robert Oppenheimer was born on April 22, 1904, to a German immigrant who was making his fortune by importing textiles in New York City. He is most remembered for his work with Albert Einstein on the first atomic bomb.

artist/company:	**Peter Aversten**
based in:	Stockholm, Sweden
artwork titles	The Nuclear Series
software used:	Pixels:3D, Photoshop, After Effects
contact info:	aversten@meshmen.com

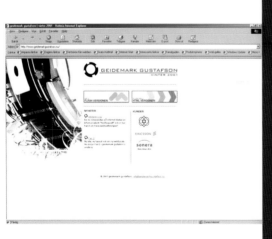

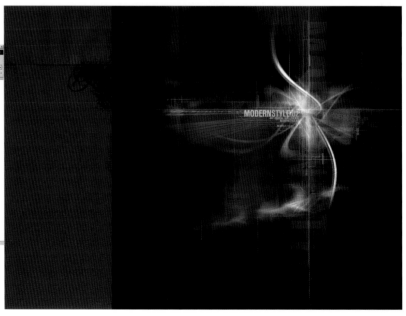

artist/company:	**Per Gustafson**
based in:	Hallstahammar, Sweden
artwork titles:	Per Gustavsson Portfolio, Modern Style, Tribute to MetalHeart, Overload, Geidemark Gustavsson
software used:	Photoshop, Flash, LightWave 3D
contact info:	per@modernstyle.nu

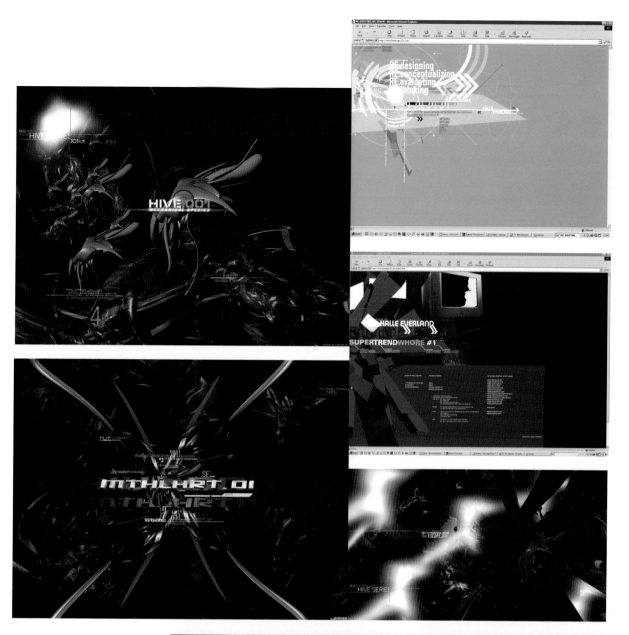

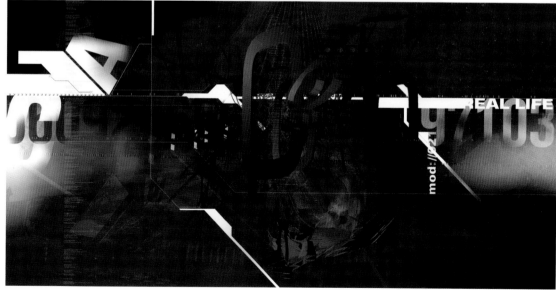

artist/company:	**Kalle Everland**
based in:	Stockholm, Sweden
artwork titles:	Hive 001, Hive 002, Hive S, Real Life, RE.Designing, SuperTrendWhore
software used:	Photoshop, 3D Studio Max
contact info:	kalle_everland@yahoo.com

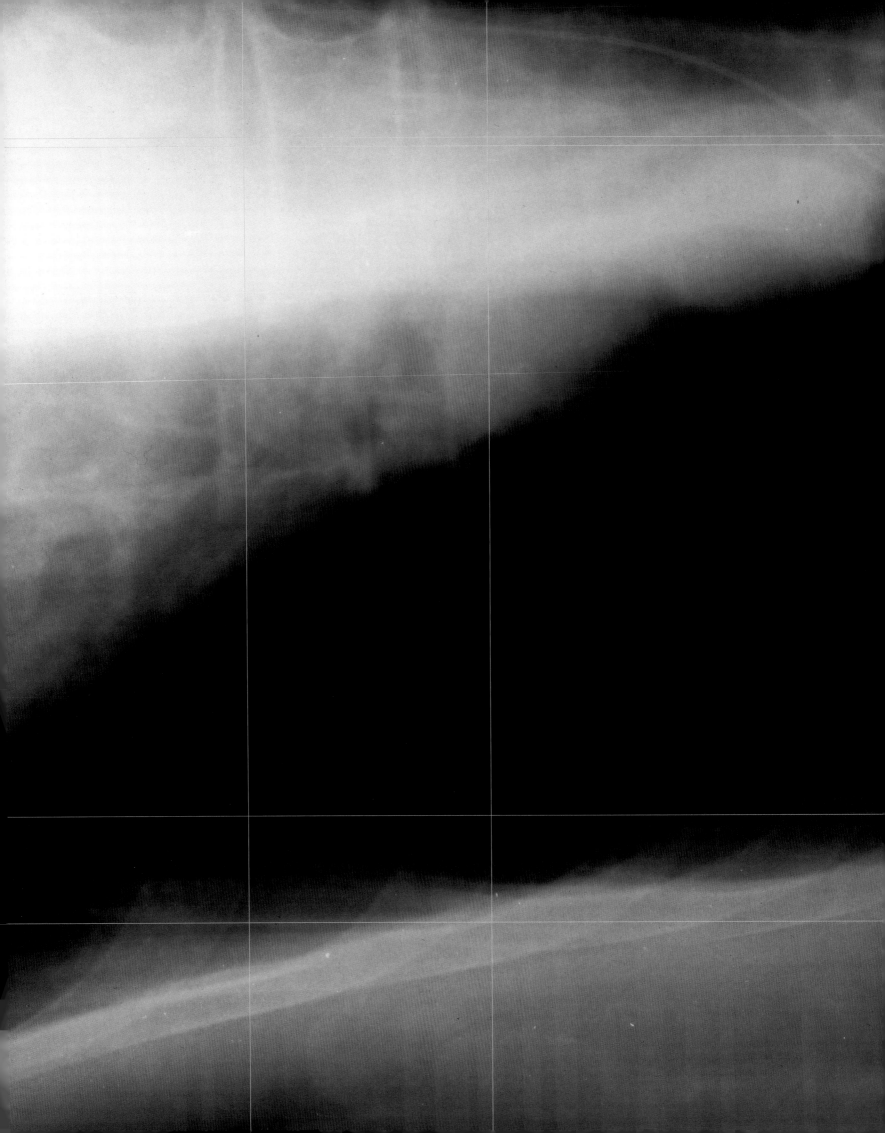

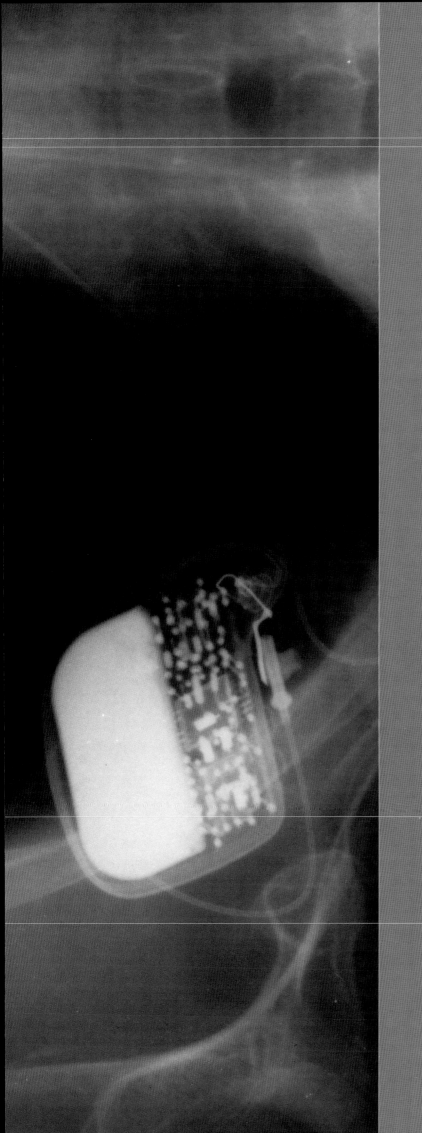

METALHEART IS MORE

MetalHeart is so much more:
animations, videos, patterns, textures, surface materials, the
MetalHeart Backgrounds, presets, and other cool libraries.
On the complementary CD we have included some of our favorite
art materials, and some tips and tricks from our archives.
But we have more to give you...
so, we guess there is bound to be another volume.

_Andreas and Anders F

artist/company:	**Bruce Reeves**	artist/company:	**Alexander Carter**
artwork title:	Tube Steal Boogie (Neutronica Poster)	artwork title:	Brainreactor Poster
software used:	Illustrator, Photoshop	software used:	Illustrator, Photoshop

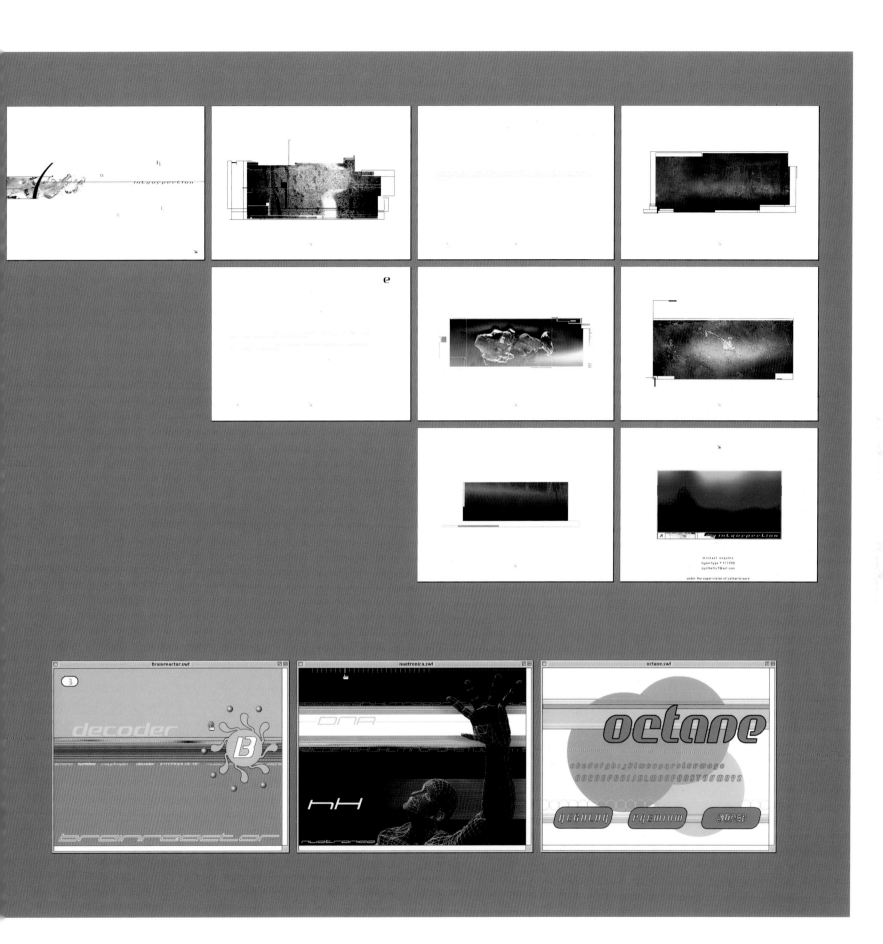

artist/company:	**Michael Esquino** (Under the supervision of Catarin Eure)
artwork title:	Introspection
software used:	Director, Illustrator, Photoshop

artist/company:	**Ian Walter**
artwork title:	Flash Pieces
software used:	Flash

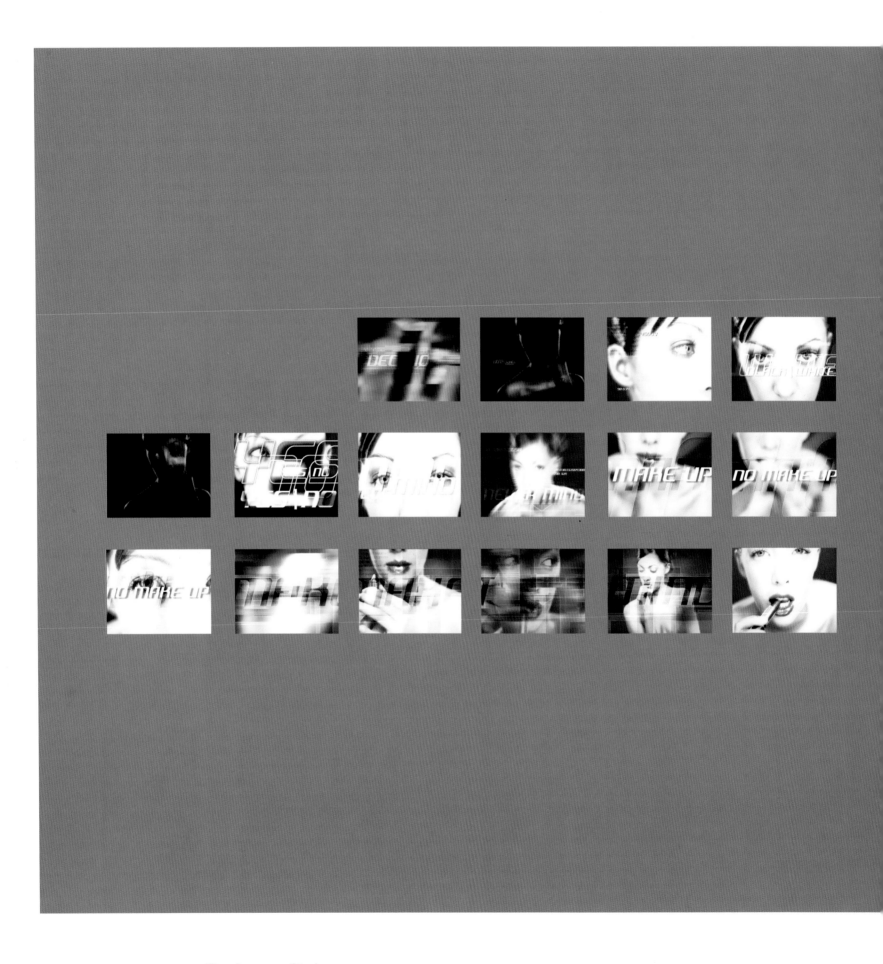

| artist/company: | **Klas Jonsson,** Strobe | software used: | After Effects, Photoshop, Avid Media Composer |
| artwork title: | Make Your Mind Up | comments: | Test spot |

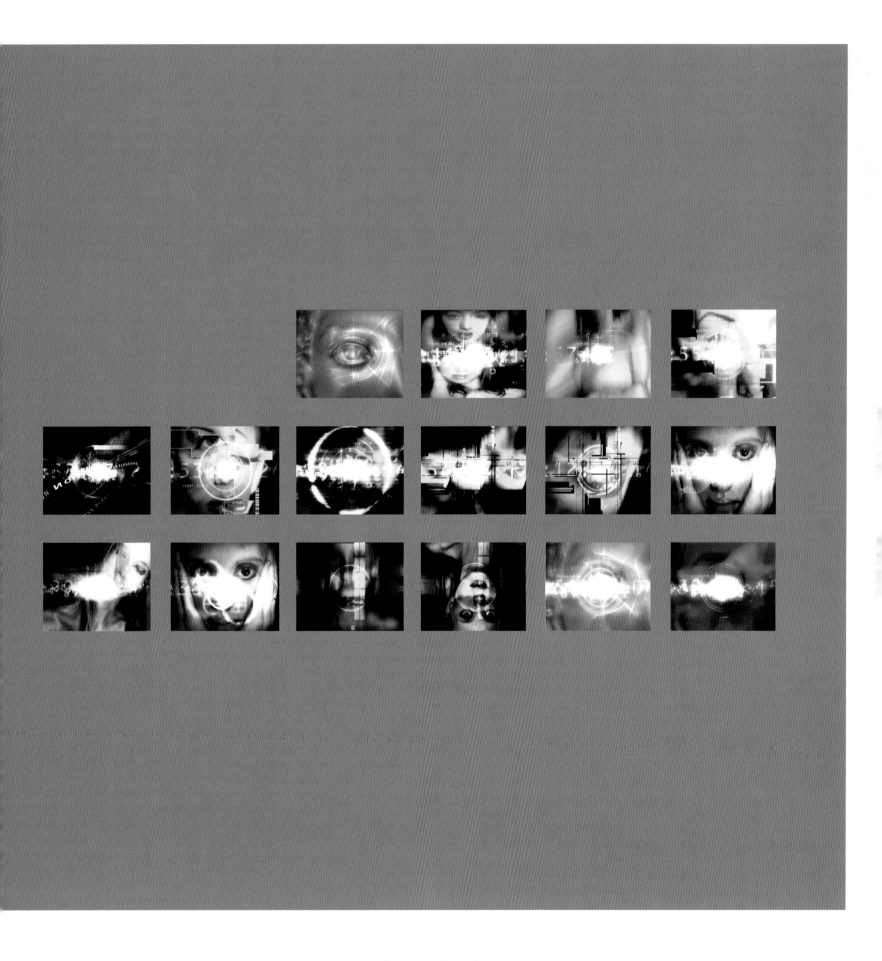

artist/company: **Klas Jonsson, Lars Heydecke, Andreas Lindholm,** Megafront

artwork title: The Millennium Movie

software used: FreeHand, Photoshop, After Effects,

Avid Media Composer

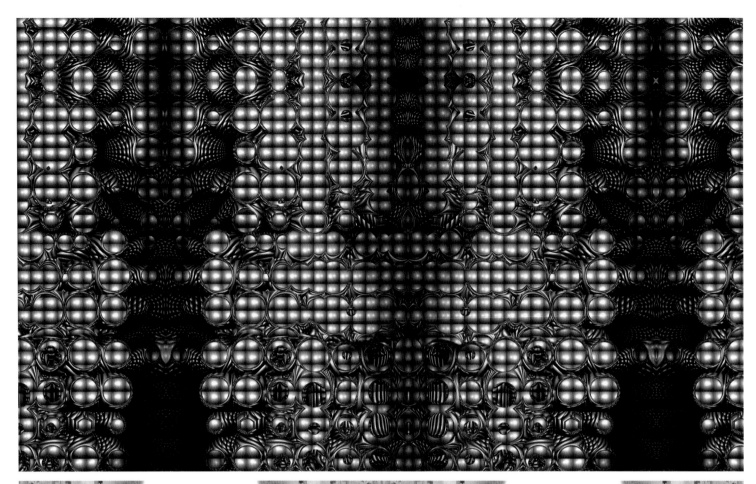

artist/company: **Anders F Rönnblom,** Studio Matchbox

artwork titles: Metal Bubbles, Terra Front, Artwork Swirls, Terrazzo Spatial Reflection

software used: Pixar Typestry, Terrazzo, Live Picture, Photoshop

comments: Images available on the complementary MetalHeart CD

artist/company:	**Anders F Rönnblom,** Studio Matchbox
artwork titles:	Terrazzo Pattern 1 & 2

software used:	Pixar Typestry, Terrazzo, Live Picture, Photoshop
comments:	Seamless tiles available on the complementary MetalHeart CD

artists: **Anders F Rönnblom and Andreas Lindholm**

artwork titles: Reconstructions 25 (from the CD-Rom collection MetalHeart Backgrounds Vol. 02: Reconstruction)

software used: FreeHand, Pixar Typestry, Photoshop, Live Picture

comments: Hi-res image (70Mb) available on the complementary MetalHeart CD

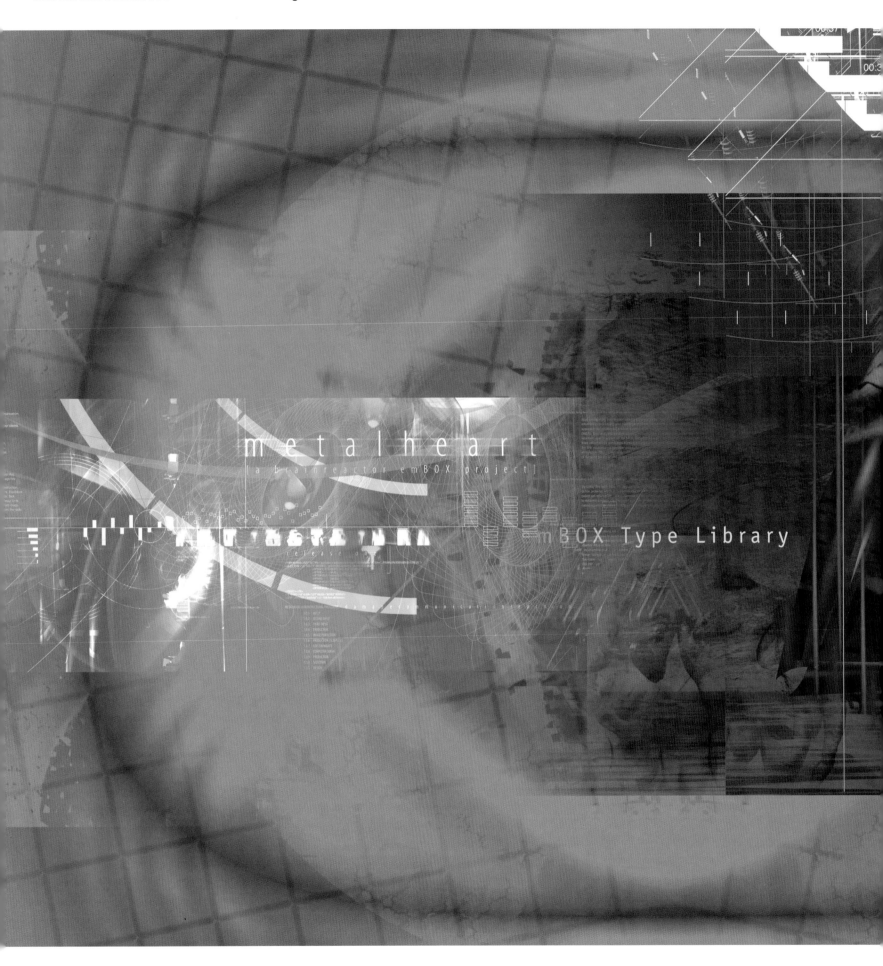

artists: **Anders F Rönnblom and Andreas Lindholm**

artwork title: Reconstruction 08 (from the CD-Rom collection MetalHeart Backgrounds Volume 02: Reconstructions)

CORRUPT METAL

software used: FreeHand, Pixar Typestry, Photoshop, Live Picture

comments: Hi-res image (70Mb) available on the complementary MetalHeart CD

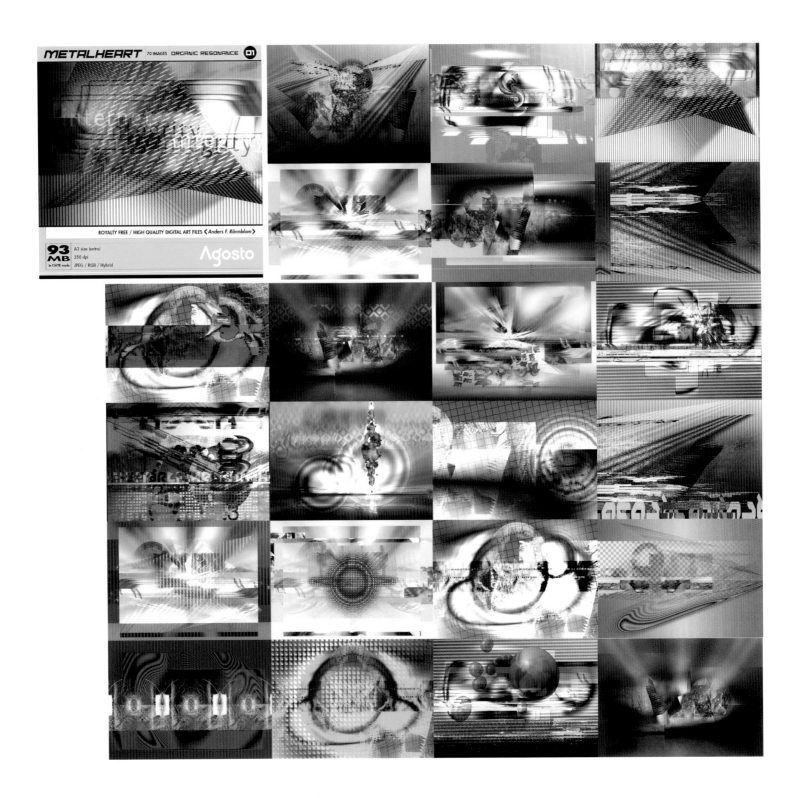

artwork title:	**The royalty-free CD-Rom collection "MetalHeart Backgrounds Volume 01: Organic Resonance "**	
designed by:	Anders F Rönnblom, Studio Matchbox	
published by:	Agosto Inc.	
contact info:	www.agosto.com	

artwork title: **The royalty-free CD-Rom collection "MetalHeart Backgrounds Volume 02: Reconstructions "**

designed by: Anders F Rönnblom & Andreas Lindholm

published by: Agosto Inc.

contact info: www.agosto.com

MetalHeart is Digital
The CD-ROM attached to the back side of this book contains all the following digital royalty-free files for your personal and professional use.

The Prototype CD :
We have included this prototype collection for those of you who missed the first shipment three years ago. Designed by Anders F Rönnblom using Pixar Typestry and RenderMan technology. Additional characters can be downloaded from: www.macartdesign.matchbox.se

emBOX_
CyberBronze

CyberBronze_A.psd

CyberBronze_B.psd

CyberBronze_C.psd

CyberBronze_D.psd

CyberBronze_E.psd

CyberBronze_F.psd

CyberBronze_G.psd

CyberBronze_H.psd

CyberBronze_I.psd

CyberBronze_J.psd

CyberBronze_K.psd

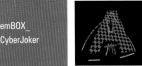
emBOX_
CyberJoker

CyberJoker_A.psd

CyberJoker_A_
b&w.psd

CyberJoker_B.psd

CyberJoker_B_
b&w.psd

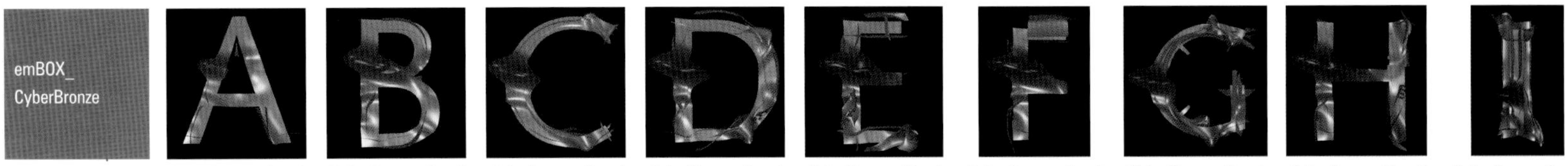

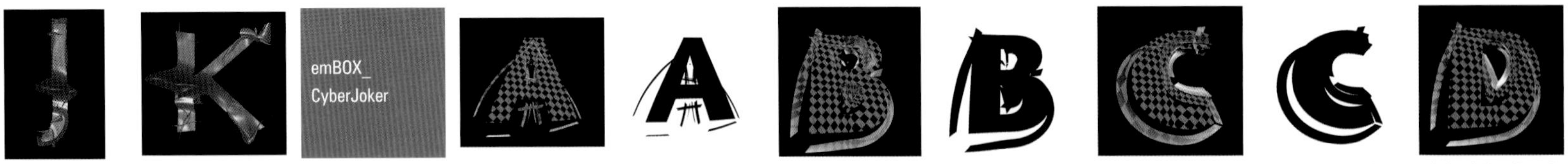

CyberJoker_C.psd

CyberJoker_C_
b&w.psd

CyberJoker_D.psd

CyberJoker_D_
b&w.psd

CyberJoker_E.psd

CyberJoker_E_
b&w.psd

CyberJoker_F.psd

CyberJoker_F_
b&w.psd

CyberJoker_G.psd

CyberJoker_G_
b&w.psd

CyberJoker_H.psd

CyberJoker_H_
b&w.psd

CyberJoker_I.psd

CyberJoker_I_
b&w.psd

CyberJoker_J.psd

CyberJoker_J_
b&w.psd

CyberJoker_K.psd

CyberJoker_K_
b&w.psd

CyberJoker_L.psd

CyberJoker_L_
b&w.psd

CyberJoker_M.psd

CyberJoker_M_
b&w.psd

CyberJoker_N.psd

CyberJoker_N_
b&w.psd

CyberJoker_O.psd

CyberJoker_O_
b&w.psd

CyberJoker_P.psd

CyberJoker_P_
b&w.psd

emBOX_
CyberMetal

CyberMetal_A.psd

CyberMetal_B.psd

CyberMetal_C.psd

CyberMetal_D.psd

CyberMetal_E.psd

CyberMetal_F.psd

CyberMetal_G.psd

CyberMetal_H.psd

CyberMetal_I.psd

CyberMetal_J.psd

CyberMetal_K.psd

CyberMetal_L.psd

CyberMetal_M.psd

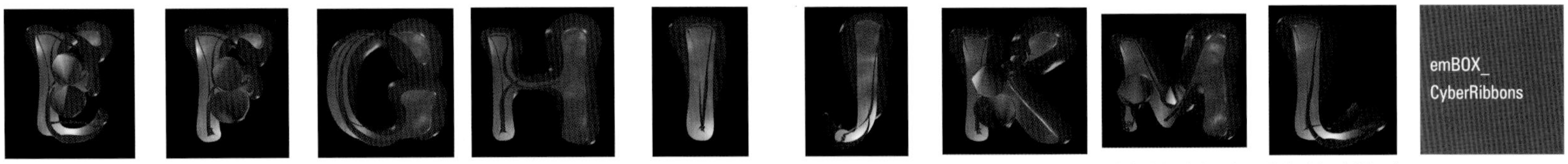

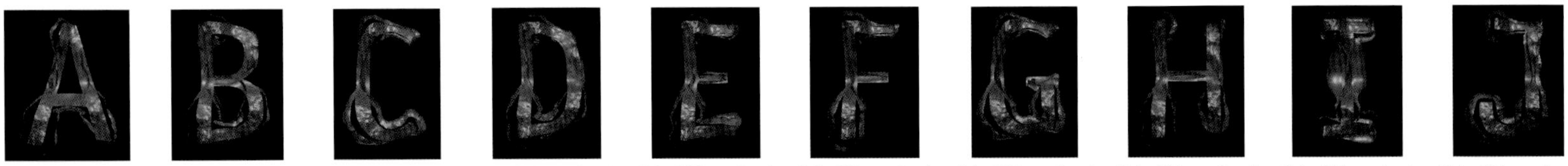

emBOX_
CyberRibbons

CyberRibbons_A.psd

CyberRibbons_B.psd

CyberRibbons_C.psd

CyberRibbons_D.psd

CyberRibbons_E.psd

CyberRibbons_F.psd

CyberRibbons_G.psd

CyberRibbons_H.psd

CyberRibbons_I.psd

CyberRibbons_J.psd

CyberRibbons_K.psd

CyberRibbons_L.psd

CyberRibbons_M.psd

CyberRibbons_N.psd

CyberRibbons_O.psd

CyberRibbons_P.psd

CyberRibbons_Q.psd

CyberRibbons_R.psd

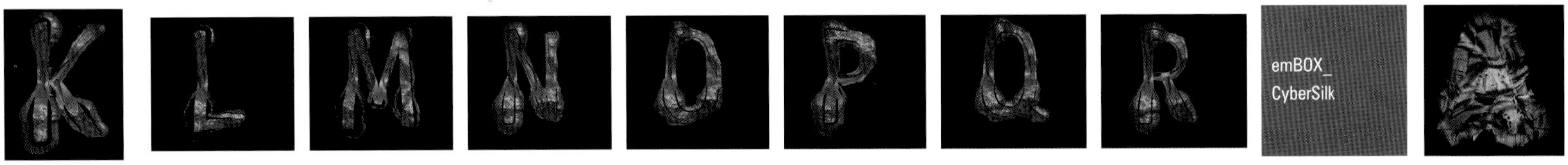

emBOX_
CyberSilk

CyberSilk_A.psd

      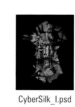  

CyberSilk_B.psd | CyberSilk_C.psd | CyberSilk_D.psd | CyberSilk_E.psd | CyberSilk_F.psd | CyberSilk_G.psd | CyberSilk_H.psd | CyberSilk_I.psd | CyberSilk_J.psd | CyberSilk_K.psd

emBOX_CyberSmoke | CyberSmoke_A.psd | CyberSmoke_B.psd | CyberSmoke_C.psd | CyberSmoke_D.psd | CyberSmoke_E.psd | CyberSmoke_F.psd | CyberSmoke_G.psd | CyberSmoke_H.psd | CyberSmoke_I.psd

 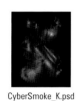      

CyberSmoke_J.psd | CyberSmoke_K.psd | emBOX_CyberSprout | CyberSprout_A.psd | CyberSprout_A_b&w.psd | CyberSprout_B.psd | CyberSprout_B_b&w.psd | CyberSprout_C.psd | CyberSprout_C_b&w.psd | CyberSprout_D.psd

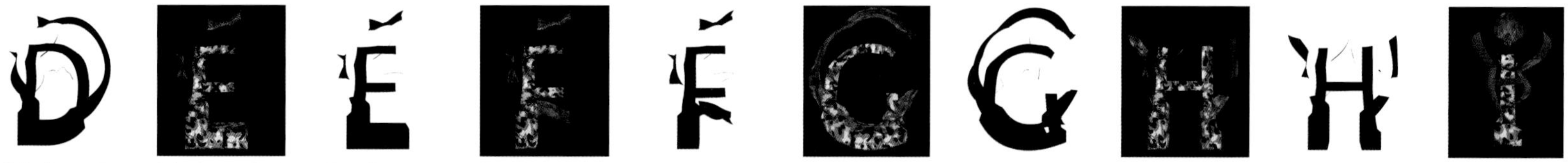

CyberSprout_D_b&w.psd | CyberSprout_E.psd | CyberSprout_E_b&w.psd | CyberSprout_F.psd | CyberSprout_F_b&w.psd | CyberSprout_G.psd | CyberSprout_G_b&w.psd | CyberSprout_H.psd | CyberSprout_H_b&w.psd | CyberSprout_I.psd

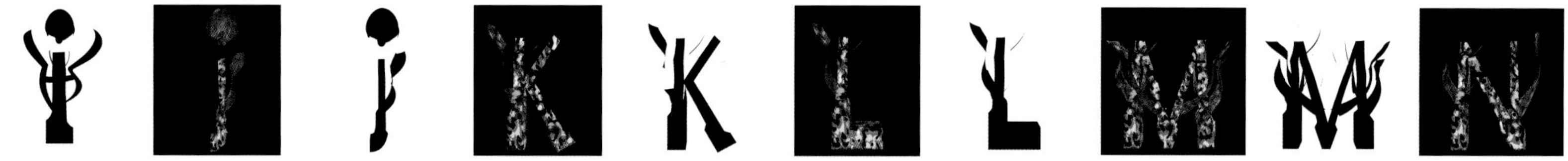

CyberSprout_I_b&w.psd | CyberSprout_J.psd | CyberSprout_J_b&w.psd | CyberSprout_K.psd | CyberSprout_K_b&w.psd | CyberSprout_L.psd | CyberSprout_L_b&w.psd | CyberSprout_M.psd | CyberSprout_M_b&w.psd | CyberSprout_N.psd

CyberSprout_N_b&w.psd | CyberSprout_O.psd | CyberSprout_O_b&w.psd | CyberSprout_P.psd | CyberSprout_P_b&w.psd | emBOX_FreakyNuclear | FreakyNuclear_A.psd | FreakyNuclear_B.psd | FreakyNuclear_C.psd | FreakyNuclear_D.psd

    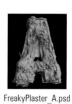  

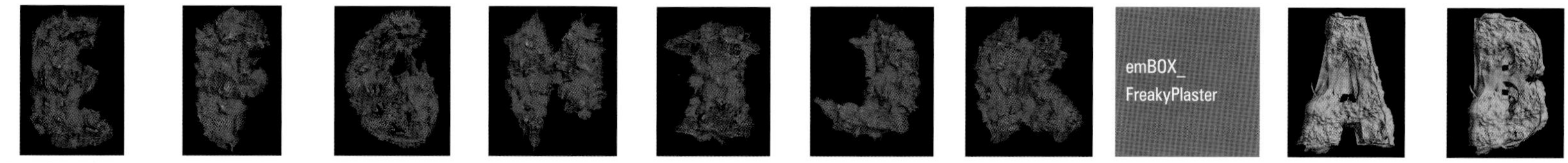

FreakyNuclear_E.psd | FreakyNuclear_F.psd | FreakyNuclear_G.psd | FreakyNuclear_H.psd | FreakyNuclear_I.psd | FreakyNuclear_J.psd | FreakyNuclear_K.psd | emBOX_FreakyPlaster | FreakyPlaster_A.psd | FreakyPlaster_B.psd

 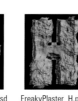     

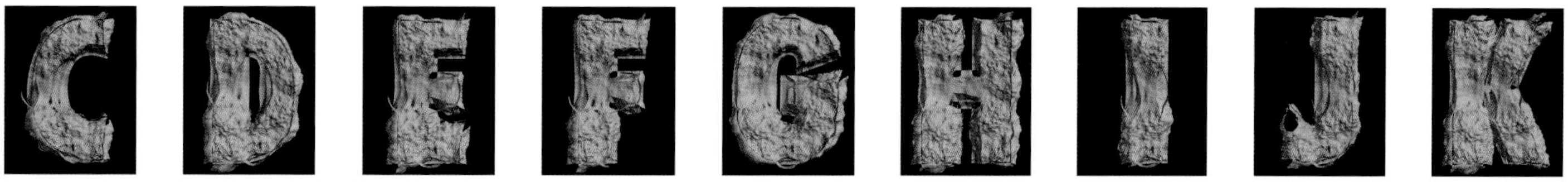

FreakyPlaster_C.psd | FreakyPlaster_D.psd | FreakyPlaster_E.psd | FreakyPlaster_F.psd | FreakyPlaster_G.psd | FreakyPlaster_H.psd | FreakyPlaster_I.psd | FreakyPlaster_J.psd | FreakyPlaster_K.psd

The emBOX Typeface Collection:

These typefaces have been rendered with RenderMan technology in Pixar Typestry 2.1.2. Each character is a 24-bit color image including an 8-bit alpha channel. The background is black in order to provide the best quality for the alpha channel mask. Please note that some images are transparent.

Some of these renderings are extremely advanced, using one of RenderMan's most powerful features – the displacemnet parameter, allowing you to displace the actual physical model of your character.

These rendered images are experiments, and some characters may be illegible and hard to identify. We have also, for some typefaces, included black and white images which can be used as complements.

The additional characters of the emBOX typefaces can be downloaded on our website   www.macartdesign.matchbox.se

emBOX Typefaces CREATED BY: Anders F Rönnblom, Stockholm, Sweden   ©1998 by Anders F Rönnblom   email: macartdesign@matchbox.se

emBOX_
CinderellaCrack

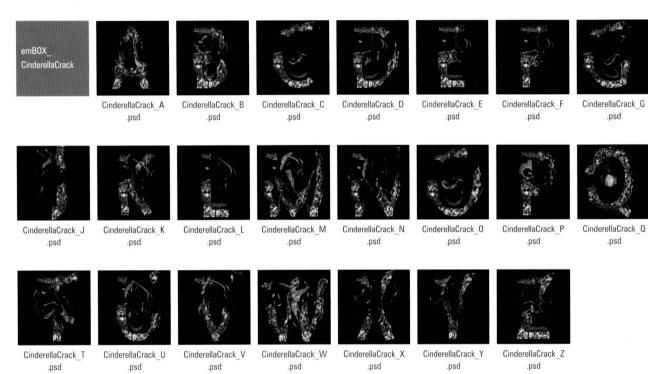

CinderellaCrack_A .psd	CinderellaCrack_B .psd	CinderellaCrack_C .psd	CinderellaCrack_D .psd	CinderellaCrack_E .psd	CinderellaCrack_F .psd	CinderellaCrack_G .psd	CinderellaCrack_H .psd	CinderellaCrack_I .psd
CinderellaCrack_J .psd	CinderellaCrack_K .psd	CinderellaCrack_L .psd	CinderellaCrack_M .psd	CinderellaCrack_N .psd	CinderellaCrack_O .psd	CinderellaCrack_P .psd	CinderellaCrack_Q .psd	CinderellaCrack_R .psd	CinderellaCrack_S .psd
CinderellaCrack_T .psd	CinderellaCrack_U .psd	CinderellaCrack_V .psd	CinderellaCrack_W .psd	CinderellaCrack_X .psd	CinderellaCrack_Y .psd	CinderellaCrack_Z .psd

emBOX_
CrystopiaJewel

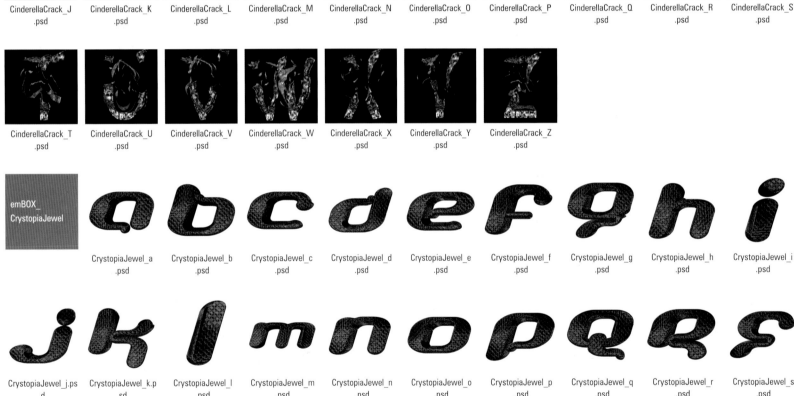

CrystopiaJewel_a .psd	CrystopiaJewel_b .psd	CrystopiaJewel_c .psd	CrystopiaJewel_d .psd	CrystopiaJewel_e .psd	CrystopiaJewel_f .psd	CrystopiaJewel_g .psd	CrystopiaJewel_h .psd	CrystopiaJewel_i .psd

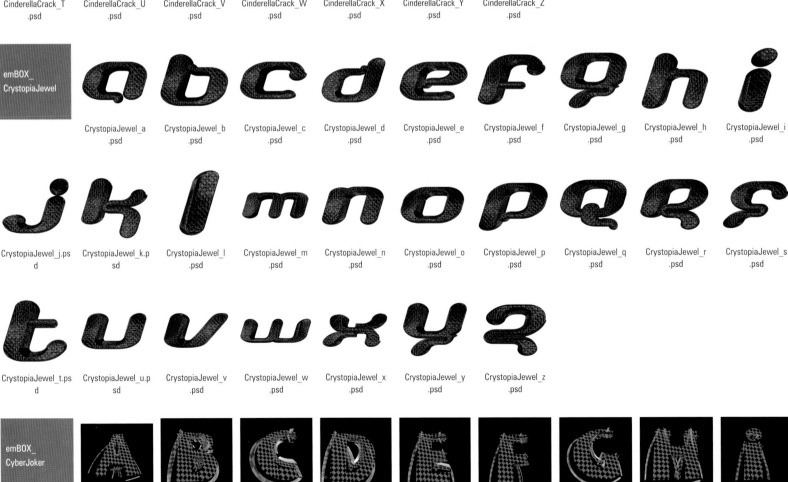

CrystopiaJewel_j.psd	CrystopiaJewel_k.psd	CrystopiaJewel_l .psd	CrystopiaJewel_m .psd	CrystopiaJewel_n .psd	CrystopiaJewel_o .psd	CrystopiaJewel_p .psd	CrystopiaJewel_q .psd	CrystopiaJewel_r .psd	CrystopiaJewel_s .psd

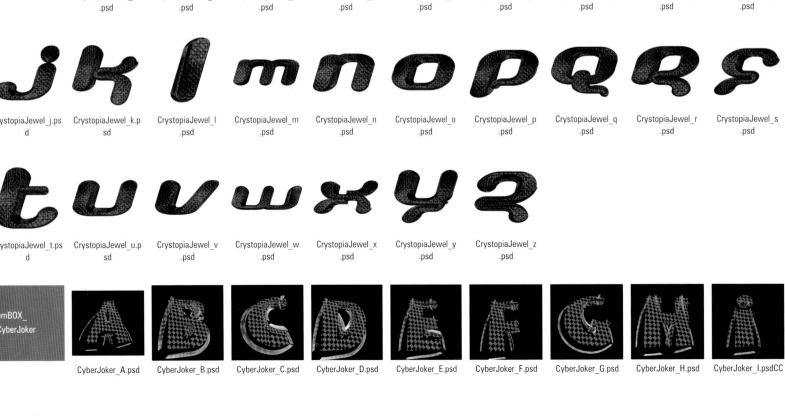

CrystopiaJewel_t.psd	CrystopiaJewel_u.psd	CrystopiaJewel_v .psd	CrystopiaJewel_w .psd	CrystopiaJewel_x .psd	CrystopiaJewel_y .psd	CrystopiaJewel_z .psd

emBOX_
CyberJoker

CyberJoker_A.psd	CyberJoker_B.psd	CyberJoker_C.psd	CyberJoker_D.psd	CyberJoker_E.psd	CyberJoker_F.psd	CyberJoker_G.psd	CyberJoker_H.psd	CyberJoker_I.psdCC

 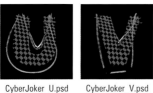 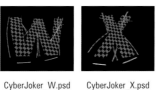

| yberJoker_J.psd | CyberJoker_K.psdy | berJoker_L.psd | CyberJoker_M.psd | CyberJoker_N.psd | CyberJoker_O.psd | CyberJoker_P.psd | CyberJoker_Q.psd | CyberJoker_R.psd | CyberJoker_S.psd |

| CyberJoker_T.psd | CyberJoker_U.psd | CyberJoker_V.psd | CyberJoker_W.psd | CyberJoker_X.psd | CyberJoker_Y.psd | CyberJoker_Z.psd |

emBOX_
CyberMetalMother

| CyberMetalMother_ A.psd | CyberMetalMother_ B.psd | CyberMetalMother_ C.psd | CyberMetalMother_ D.psd | CyberMetalMother_ E.psd | CyberMetalMother_ F.psd | CyberMetalMother_ G.psd | CyberMetalMother_ H.psd | CyberMetalMother_ I.psd |

| CyberMetalMother_ J.psd | CyberMetalMother_ K.psd | CyberMetalMother_ L.psd | CyberMetalMother_ M.psd | CyberMetalMother_ N.psd | CyberMetalMother_ O.psd | CyberMetalMother_ P.psd | CyberMetalMother_ Q.psd | CyberMetalMother_ R.psd | CyberMetalMother_ S.psd |

       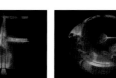

| CyberMetalMother_ T.psd | CyberMetalMother_ U.psd | CyberMetalMother_ V.psd | CyberMetalMother_ W.psd | CyberMetalMother_ X.psd | CyberMetalMother_ Y.psd | CyberMetalMother_ Z.psd |

emBOX_
CyberSmoke

  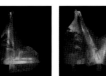

| CyberSmoke_A.psd | CyberSmoke_B.psd | CyberSmoke_C.psd | CyberSmoke_D.psd | CyberSmoke_E.psd | CyberSmoke_F.psd | CyberSmoke_G.psd | CyberSmoke_H.psd | CyberSmoke_I.psd |

       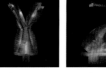

| CyberSmoke_J.psd | CyberSmoke_K.psd | CyberSmoke_L.psd | CyberSmoke_M.psd | CyberSmoke_N.psd | CyberSmoke_O.psd | CyberSmoke_P.psd | CyberSmoke_Q.psd | CyberSmoke_R.psd | CyberSmoke_S.psd |

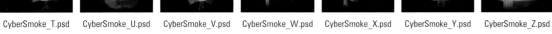

| CyberSmoke_T.psd | CyberSmoke_U.psd | CyberSmoke_V.psd | CyberSmoke_W.psd | CyberSmoke_X.psd | CyberSmoke_Y.psd | CyberSmoke_Z.psd |

emBOX_
Ind_Faith_Unfaith

Ind_Faith_Unfaith_a
.psd

Ind_Faith_Unfaith_b
.psd

Ind_Faith_Unfaith_c
.psd

Ind_Faith_Unfaith_d
.psd

Ind_Faith_Unfaith_e
.psd

Ind_Faith_Unfaith_f
.psd

Ind_Faith_Unfaith_g
.psd

Ind_Faith_Unfaith_h
.psd

Ind_Faith_Unfaith_i
.psd

Ind_Faith_Unfaith_j
.psd

Ind_Faith_Unfaith_k
.psd

Ind_Faith_Unfaith_l
.psd

Ind_Faith_Unfaith_m
.psd

Ind_Faith_Unfaith_n
.psd

Ind_Faith_Unfaith_o
.psd

Ind_Faith_Unfaith_p
.psd

Ind_Faith_Unfaith_q
.psd

Ind_Faith_Unfaith_r
.psd

Ind_Faith_Unfaith_s
.psd

Ind_Faith_Unfaith_t
.psd

Ind_Faith_Unfaith_u
.psd

Ind_Faith_Unfaith_v
.psd

Ind_Faith_Unfaith_w
.psd

Ind_Faith_Unfaith_x
.psd

Ind_Faith_Unfaith_y
.psd

Ind_Faith_Unfaith_z
.psd

emBOX_
React_Ornament

React_Ornam_a.psd

React_Ornam_b.psd

React_Ornam_c.psd

React_Ornam_d.psd

React_Ornam_e.psd

React_Ornam_f.psd

React_Ornam_g.psd

React_Ornam_h.psd

React_Ornam_i.psd

React_Ornam_j.psd

React_Ornam_k.psd

React_Ornam_l.psd

React_Ornam_m.psd

React_Ornam_n.psd

React_Ornam_o.psd

React_Ornam_p.psd

React_Ornam_q.psd

React_Ornam_r.psd

React_Ornam_s.psd

React_Ornam_t.psd

React_Ornam_u.psd

React_Ornam_v.psd

React_Ornam_w.psd

React_Ornam_x.psd

React_Ornam_y.psd

React_Ornam_z.psd

MetalHeart Backgrounds:

The MetalHeart Backgrounds, published by Agosto Inc., are royaltyfree digital art images of a very high quality. Each 300 dpi image has an approximate file size of 70Mb in RGB mode (93Mb in CMYK) and includes graphic elements designed by Anders F Rönnblom and Andreas Lindholm. From the 2 first collections, Organic Resonance and Reconstructions, we give you 6 images free, for you to use for print, video, multimedia or web design. 10 more collections are in the works, to be published later in 2001.For more information: www.agosto.com

MH_Organic
Resonance08.jpg

MH_Organic
Resonance22.jpg

MH_Organic
Resonance58.jpg

MH_Reconstruction
08.jpg

MH_Reconstruction
25.jpg

MH_Reconstruction
56.jpg

MetalHeart Gradients:
This is a collection of 15 big gradient images (25Mb) which could be used as is, for decorative high res graphic design, or as grayscale images in various alpha channel processes for 72 dpi screen design. Designed by Anders F Rönnblom, Studio Matchbox.

| MetalGRADIENT_01 .jpg | MetalGRADIENT_02 .jpg | MetalGRADIENT_03 .jpg | MetalGRADIENT_04 .jpg | MetalGRADIENT_05 .jpg | MetalGRADIENT_06 .jpg | MetalGRADIENT_07 .jpg | MetalGRADIENT_08 .jpg | MetalGRADIENT_09 .jpg | MetalGRADIENT_10 .jpg |

| MetalGRADIENT_11 .jpg | MetalGRADIENT_12 .jpg | MetalGRADIENT_13 .jpg | MetalGRADIENT_14 .jpg | MetalGRADIENT_15 .jpg |

MetalHeart Patterns:
This is a collection of 10 high resolution patterns (approx. file size: 30Mb). Designed by Anders F Rönnblom, Studio Matchbox.

| MetalPATTERN_01 .jpg | MetalPATTERN_02 .jpg | MetalPATTERN_03 .jpg | MetalPATTERN_04 .jpg | MetalPATTERN_05 .jpg | MetalPATTERN_06 .jpg | MetalPATTERN_07 .jpg | MetalPATTERN_08 .jpg | MetalPATTERN_09 .jpg | MetalPATTERN_10 .jpg |

MetalHeart Tiles:
This is a collection of 28 high resolution seamless tiles (4.25Mb), to be defined as patterns in Photoshop and used as attractive tiled backgrounds. Designed by Anders F Rönnblom, Studio Matchbox.

| MetalTILE_01.jpg | MetalTILE_02.jpg | MetalTILE_03.jpg | MetalTILE_04.jpg | MetalTILE_05.jpg | MetalTILE_06.jpg | MetalTILE_07.jpg | MetalTILE_08.jpg | MetalTILE_09.jpg | MetalTILE_10.jpg |

| MetalTILE_11.jpg | MetalTILE_12.jpg | MetalTILE_13.jpg | MetalTILE_14.jpg | MetalTILE_15.jpg | MetalTILE_16.jpg | MetalTILE_17.jpg | MetalTILE_18.jpg | MetalTILE_19.jpg | MetalTILE_20.jpg |

    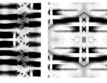

| MetalTILE_21.jpg | MetalTILE_22.jpg | MetalTILE_23.jpg | MetalTILE_24.jpg | MetalTILE_25.jpg | MetalTILE_26.jpg | MetalTILE_27.jpg | MetalTILE_28.jpg |

MetalHeart/Meshmen Textures:

These are 99 textures created by Peter Aversten and Fredrik Fogelqvist of the Meshmen group in Örebro, Sweden. The textures are true studies of nature and a report of what's left of the Kvarntorp industrial area outside the city of Örebro. The collection includes Bark, Bult, Clay, Concrete, Grass, Grounds, Metals, Moss, Planks, Plates, Slate, Tire, Walls, and several variations of Rusts.

MH_MM_Bark .jpg	MH_MM_Bult01 .jpg	MH_MM_Bult02 .jpg	MH_MM_Clay01 .jpg	MH_MM_Clay02 .jpg	MH_MM_Clay03 .jpg	MH_MM_Clay04 .jpg	MH_MM_Concrete .jpg	MH_MM_Fungus .jpg	MH_MM_Grass .jpg
MH_MM_Ground01 .jpg	MH_MM_Ground02 .jpg	MH_MM_Ground03 .jpg	MH_MM_Ground04 .jpg	MH_MM_Ground05 .jpg	MH_MM_Ground06 .jpg	MH_MM_Ground07 .jpg	MH_MM_Ground08 .jpg	MH_MM_Ground09 .jpg	MH_MM_Ground10 .jpg
MH_MM_Ground11 .jpg	MH_MM_Ground12 .jpg	MH_MM_Ground13 .jpg	MH_MM_Ground14 .jpg	MH_MM_Ground15 .jpg	MH_MM_Ground16 .jpg	MH_MM_Ground17 .jpg	MH_MM_Ground18 .jpg	MH_MM_Ground19 .jpg	MH_MM_Ground20 .jpg
MH_MM_Ground21 .jpg	MH_MM_Metal01 .jpg	MH_MM_Metal02 .jpg	MH_MM_Metal03 .jpg	MH_MM_Metal04 .jpg	MH_MM_Metal05 .jpg	MH_MM_Metal06 .jpg	MH_MM_Moss01 .jpg	MH_MM_Moss02 .jpg	MH_MM_Moss03 .jpg
MH_MM_Paint01 .jpg	MH_MM_Paint02 .jpg	MH_MM_Planks01 .jpg	MH_MM_Planks02 .jpg	MH_MM_Plate01 .jpg	MH_MM_Plate02 .jpg	MH_MM_Plate03 .jpg	MH_MM_Rubber01 .jpg	MH_MM_Rubber02 .jpg	MH_MM_Rubber03 .jpg
MH_MM_Rubber04 .jpg	MH_MM_Rubber05 .jpg	MH_MM_Rubber06 .jpg	MH_MM_Rubber07 .jpg	MH_MM_Rust01 .jpg	MH_MM_Rust02 .jpg	MH_MM_Rust03 .jpg	MH_MM_Rust04 .jpg	MH_MM_Rust05 .jpg	MH_MM_Rust06 .jpg
MH_MM_Rust07 .jpg	MH_MM_Rust08 .jpg	MH_MM_Rust09 .jpg	MH_MM_Rust10 .jpg	MH_MM_Rust11 .jpg	MH_MM_Rust12 .jpg	MH_MM_Rust13 .jpg	MH_MM_Rust14 .jpg	MH_MM_Rust15 .jpg	MH_MM_Rust16 .jpg
MH_MM_Rust17 .jpg	MH_MM_Rust18 .jpg	MH_MM_Rust19 .jpg	MH_MM_Rust20 .jpg	MH_MM_Rust21 .jpg	MH_MM_Rust22 .jpg	MH_MM_Rust23 .jpg	MH_MM_Rust24 .jpg	MH_MM_Rust25 .jpg	MH_MM_Rust26 .jpg

| MH_MM_Rust27 .jpg | MH_MM_Rust28 .jpg | MH_MM_Rust29 .jpg | MH_MM_Rust30 .jpg | MH_MM_Rust31 .jpg | MH_MM_Slate01 .jpg | MH_MM_Slate02 .jpg | MH_MM_Slate03 .jpg | MH_MM_Slate04 .jpg | MH_MM_Slate05 .jpg |

| MH_MM_ Stoneground.jpg | MH_MM_ Sulphur.jpg | MH_MM_Sulphur ground01.jpg | MH_MM_Sulphur ground02.jpg | MH_MM_Tire.jpg | MH_MM_Wall01 .jpg | MH_MM_Wall02 .jpg | MH_MM_ Wetground01.jpg | MH_MM_ Wetground02.jpg |

The emBOX Slide Show:
A slide show including rendered images of emBOX typefaces and Brainreactor fonts. Created by Anders F Rönnblom.

Movies and Animations
"Introspection" A multimedia project by Michel Esquino, student at the Art Institute of Southern California, Laguna Beach (under the supervision of Catarin Eure).
"Make Your Mind Up" Commercial test spot by KLAS JONSSON, Strobe. "The Millennium Movie" Promotional film to back up the Millennium Calendar project. By Klas Jonsson, Lars Heydecke and Andreas Lindholm, Megafront.

The Brainreactor Fonts:

These are the original Techno fonts designed by Andreas Lindholm. These are conventional fonts, that you install in your system and use in your graphic application by typing with your keyboard. When you cannot install them directly from CD-ROM, drag and copy the folders or files to your desktop first and install the copied ones to your machine.
Brainreactor Fonts CREATED BY: Andreas Lindholm, Stockholm, Sweden   ©1998 Andreas Lindholm   email: andreas@megafront.com

399 Missile-Normal
[MAC ONLY]

399 Missile-Thin
[MAC ONLY]

Amraam-Heavy
[MAC ONLY]

Amraam-Medium
[MAC ONLY]

Amraam-Thin
[MAC ONLY]

Bumblebee on acid
[MAC & WIN]

Bumblebee on the moon
[MAC ONLY]

Crystopia Atmosphere
[MAC & WIN]

Crystopia Ultraspace
[MAC ONLY]

Decoder Regular
[MAC & WIN]

Decoder Thin
[MAC ONLY]

Intergalactic Highway
[MAC & WIN]

Intergalactic Veloudrome
[MAC ONLY]

Neutronica DNA
[MAC ONLY]

Neutronica Geometric
[MAC ONLY]

Neutronica outthere
[MAC ONLY]

Neutronica subspace
[MAC ONLY]

Neutronica subworld
[MAC & WIN]

Octane Premium
[MAC ONLY]

Octane Regular
[MAC ONLY]

Octane Super
[MAC & WIN]

Pornomania Peepshow
[MAC ONLY]

Pornomania Regular
[MAC & WIN]
abcdefghijklmnopqrstuvwxyz

AEROSPACER
[MAC & WIN]
AbCdEFGHIjKLMNOPNRSLUVWXYZ

CALCULATOR
[MAC & WIN]
abcdefghijklmnopqrstuvwxyz

ELASTICA
[MAC & WIN]
ABCDEFGHIJKLMNOPQRSTUVWXYZ

FUTUREMARK
[MAC & WIN]
abcdefghijklmnopqrstuvwxyz

INDUSTRIAL FAITH
[MAC & WIN]
ABCDEFGHIJKLMNOPQRSTUVWXYZ

NEODREAMS
[MAC & WIN]
AbCdEFGHIJvLMNOPQRSEUVWXYZ

PRENOPTICA
[MAC & WIN]
ABCEEFGHIJKLMNOPQRSTUVWXYZ

PROLOGIK
[MAC & WIN]
abcdefghijklmnopqrstuvwxyz

REACTIVATOR
[MAC & WIN]
abcdefghijklmnopqrstuvwxyz

ULTIMATE SURVIVAL
[MAC ONLY]
ABCDEFGHIJKLMNOPQRSTUVWXYZ

VIRUS
[MAC & WIN]
abCdeFGHIJKLMNOPQRSTUVWXYZ

Dominator-Black
[MAC ONLY]
ABCDEFGHIJHLMNOPQRSTUVWHYZ
abcdefghijhlmnopqrstuvwhyz

Dominator-BlackItalic
[MAC ONLY]
ABCDEFGHIJHLMNOPQRSTUVWHYZ
abcdefghijhlmnopqrstuvwhyz

Dominator-Medium
[MAC ONLY]
ABCDEFGHIJHLMNOPQRSTUVWHYZ
abcdefghijhlmnopqrstuvwhyz

Dominator-MediumItalic
[MAC ONLY]
ABCDEFGHIJHLMNOPQRSTUVWHYZ
abcdefghijhlmnopqrstuvwhyz

Dominator-Thin
[MAC ONLY]
ABCDEFGHIJHLMNOPQRSTUVWHYZ
abcdefghijhlmnopqrstuvwhyz

Dominator-ThinItalic
[MAC ONLY]
ABCDEFGHIJHLMNOPQRSTUVWHYZ
abcdefghijhlmnopqrstuvwhyz

Ripoff_STYLE-Normal
[MAC & WIN]
abcdefghijklmnopqrstuvwxyz

Ripoff_STYLE-Thin
[MAC & WIN]
abcdefghijklmnopqrstuvwxyz

Vaccubomb-Italic
[MAC ONLY]
ABCDEFGHIJHLMNOPQRSTUVWHYZ

Vaccubomb-Normal
[MAC ONLY]
ABCDEFGHIJHLMNOPQRSTUVWHYZ

Viagra
[MAC & WIN]
abcdefghijklmnopqrstuvwxyz

MetalHeart: **Miscellaneous – Acknowledgements**

Andreas would like to thank the following persons and companies:

Lars Lindholm (the man behind the x-rays)

Röntgenarkivet, Björkskatan Luleå

Tension Graphics, Sweden

Megafront, Sweden

Klas Tauberman, Norrköping, Sweden

Lars Heydecke, Stockholm, Sweden

Klas Jonsson, Strobe, Sweden

Henrik Larsson, Vinter Reklambyrå, Sweden

Lotta Siwertz, Stockholm, Sweden

Torbjörn Persson, Stockholm, Sweden

Eva-Lena Degerhäll, Stockholm, Sweden

Jens Karlsson, chapter3.net

Reklam Journalen, Boden, Sweden

Federico Pepe, McCann Ericson, Milano

Halvor & Torgeir, Union Design, Oslo

Avanti Färgstudio, Stockholm, Sweden

Ted Grass, unrealdynamics.com

Jimmy Hassel, 3D Festival A/S

Electronic Music producers around the world

Computer Arts mag. for their royalty free images...

+friends, colleagues and clients...

Anders F would like to thank the following persons and companies:

Ichiro Hirose, Agosto Inc, Tokyo

Rico Komanoya, DesignEXchange, Tokyo

Mariann Eklund, Studio Matchbox, Stockholm

Åke Nordgren, Avanti, Stockholm

Claude Szwimer, Paris

Stefan Larsson, GDL Technology, Budapest

Jimmy Hassel, 3D Festival, Malmö

Pixar, for the RenderMan technology

Bruno Delean, for Live Picture

Mark Zimmer, for Painter

The FUSE library, for inspiration

Edward de Bono, for lateral thinking

Richard Brautigan, for the way of saying things

The Randomizer Says, for assistance

and last but not least...

All the participant artists and designers from around the world

A big thanks also to the

EFX Art & Design publication,

for making a lot of things possible.

Andreas Lindholm can be reached at: **andreas@abstructure.com**

Anders F Rönnblom can be reached at: **macartdesign@matchbox.se**